Daily Skill Builders:

Grammar

Grades 5–6

By
CINDY BARDEN

COPYRIGHT © 2007 Mark Twain Media, Inc.

ISBN 978-1-58037-404-0

Printing No. CD-404063

Mark Twain Media, Inc., Publishers
Distributed by Carson-Dellosa Publishing Company, Inc.

Table of Contents

Table of Contents (cont.)

Introduction to the Teacher

Grammar involves learning the rules of how words are combined to form sentences. It includes understanding the relationship of words to other words, using the correct words, and using the correct forms of words (singular/plural nouns and verbs, pronoun gender, verb tense, positives, comparatives, and superlatives of adjectives and adverbs, possessive case, etc.) in the correct order.

The sentence is the basic element of both oral and written communication. Not only can changing a word completely change the entire meaning of the sentence (Example 1), but changing the order of words can also change its meaning drastically (Example 2).

Example 1: The baby is asleep.
The baby is awake.
Example 2: Sarah bit the dog.
The dog bit Sarah.

Correct capitalization and punctuation are also an interrelated and important part of proper grammatical usage essential for students to communicate effectively in writing.

A simple thing like the placement of a comma (Example 3) or addition of quotation marks (Example 4) can radically change the meaning of a sentence.

Example 3: Dr. Jones, the patient arrived an hour ago.
Dr. Jones, the patient, arrived an hour ago.
Example 4: The coach admitted his star player was unhappy after yesterday's game.
"The coach," admitted his star player, "was unhappy after yesterday's game."

Books in the *Daily Skill Builders: Grammar* series are designed to increase students' ability to use correct grammar both orally and in written communications in their schoolwork and in their everyday lives. As students develop their knowledge and understanding of grammatical usage, punctuation, and capitalization, their ability to communicate verbally and in writing will also improve. Encourage students to use dictionaries, thesauruses, and other reference sources when working on activities. After all, a student can't use a word correctly if he or she does not know its meaning.

Topics Covered

The activities in this book focus on skills that enable students to:
- identify the basic parts of speech and use them correctly in sentences;
- practice sentence-writing skills;
- form singular and plural nouns and verbs;
- form singular and plural possessive forms of nouns and pronouns;
- form present, past, and future tense of regular and irregular verbs;
- match nouns and pronouns in gender, case, and number;

Introduction to the Teacher (cont.)

- choose the correct homophone;
- choose the correct word between pairs of words often confused;
- recognize, write, and use compound words and contractions;
- differentiate between subjective, objective, and possessive pronouns and use the correct form;
- write synonyms and antonyms for words;
- recognize that some words can be more than one part of speech;
- become familiar with idioms and proverbs;
- write positives, comparatives, and superlatives of adjectives and adverbs;
- write complete sentences with subjects and predicates in agreement;
- use correct punctuation and capitalization.

Suggestions for Use

Each activity page is divided into two reproducible sections that can be cut apart and used separately. Activities could be used in class as warm-ups or for review either with a group or individually. Transparencies of the activities can encourage student participation as they follow along when a new concept is introduced. Extra copies can be kept in your learning center for review and additional practice, or copies can be distributed as homework assignments.

Organization

Activities are arranged by skill level and topic and are progressively more difficult. Activities build on knowledge covered earlier in the book.

Since standardized testing is an important component of education, review activities provide practice in standardized test-taking formats. This helps students become familiar and comfortable with the format and provides test-taking practice.

The table of contents identifies the skills that students use to complete each activity. Review pages reinforce what students learned. An answer key is provided at the end of the book.

Standards matrixes for selected states are provided on pages vi–viii. These give teachers the specific reading, writing, and language convention standards that are covered by each activity in this book. A list of the National ELA Standards as supported by NCTE and IRA can be found at [http://www.ncte.org/about/over/standards/110846.htm].

California Standards Matrix for Grades 5–6

LANGUAGE ARTS STANDARDS	ACTIVITIES
READING	
Identify and interpret figurative language and words with multiple meanings.	109, 110
Understand and explain frequently used synonyms, antonyms, and homographs.	74, 111, 113, 114, 115, 116, 117, 118, 119, 120, 121, 122, 123, 124
Use word, sentence, and paragraph clues to determine meaning of unknown words.	2, 3, 5, 6, 7, 8, 11, 12, 13, 14, 15, 20, 21, 23, 24, 25, 26, 35, 36, 39, 40, 41, 42, 43, 44, 46, 49, 50, 51, 52, 53, 54, 55, 56, 57, 58, 59, 61, 62, 63, 66, 69, 70, 72, 73, 75, 81, 82, 85, 86, 88, 101, 102, 103, 105, 106, 107, 126, 127, 138
Identify the structural features of popular media (e.g., newspapers, magazines, online information) and use the features to obtain information.	26, 75, 127
Analyze text that uses an organizational pattern (e.g., sequential or chronological order, compare and contrast).	77
WRITING	
Write personal and formal letters, letters to the editor, reviews, and poems.	136, 144
Write narratives that establish a plot, point of view, setting, conflict, and use narrative devices (e.g., dialogue, suspense).	80
Write responses to literature that demonstrate an understanding of a literary work, support judgments through references to the text and to prior knowledge, and develop interpretations.	154
Write expository compositions (e.g., description, explanation, comparison and contrast, problem and solution) that state the thesis, follow an organizational pattern appropriate to the type of composition, and offer persuasive evidence to validate arguments and conclusions as needed.	140
LANGUAGE CONVENTIONS	
Use simple, compound, and compound-complex sentences; use effective coordination and subordination of ideas to express complete thoughts.	1, 4, 16, 17, 18, 19, 30, 33, 46, 47, 48, 49, 54, 55, 60, 64, 68, 78, 79, 83, 84, 87, 92, 96, 98, 103, 108, 109, 112, 121, 122, 127, 128, 158
Identify and properly use indefinite pronouns and present perfect, past perfect, and future perfect verb tenses; ensure that verbs agree with compound subjects.	8, 9, 10, 11, 12, 14, 22, 27, 28, 29, 31, 32, 33, 34
Use colons after the salutation in business letters, semicolons to connect independent clauses, and commas when linking two clauses with a conjunction in compound sentences.	147, 148, 149, 150
Use correct capitalization.	1, 4, 17, 30, 33, 36, 68, 129, 130, 131, 132, 133, 134, 135, 136, 141, 142, 144, 158, 159, 160
Spell roots, affixes, contractions, and syllable constructions correctly.	10, 11, 12, 14, 23, 24, 25, 26, 27, 28, 29, 30, 31, 32, 33, 34, 35, 45, 60, 64, 66, 68, 71, 95, 96, 97, 98, 99, 104, 155, 156

Florida Standards Matrix for Grades 5–6

LANGUAGE ARTS STANDARDS	ACTIVITIES
READING	
Study word parts and meanings consistently across curricular content (e.g., affixes, multiple meaning words, antonyms, synonyms, root words, homonyms, homophones).	10, 23, 24, 25, 29, 35, 64, 66, 71, 88, 109, 110, 111, 113, 114, 115, 116, 117, 118, 119, 120, 121, 122, 123, 124, 125, 126, 127, 128
Use resources (e.g., dictionary, thesaurus, encyclopedia, Web sites) to clarify word meanings.	23, 24, 25, 26, 29, 31, 32, 33, 34, 64, 65, 67, 68, 74, 89, 98, 99, 107, 108, 109, 110, 111, 113, 114, 115, 116, 117, 118, 119, 120, 121, 122, 123, 124, 126, 127, 128, 137, 155, 161, 162
Use a variety of strategies to monitor texts (e.g., rereading, self-correcting, summarizing, checking other sources, using context and word structure clues).	11, 12, 14, 16, 18, 20, 21, 22, 26, 35, 39, 40, 41, 42, 43, 44, 46, 48, 50, 51, 56, 57, 58, 59, 61, 62, 63, 65, 66, 69, 70, 72, 73, 75, 81, 82, 85, 86, 91, 94, 95, 99, 100, 101, 102, 105, 106, 107, 145, 146, 147, 150, 159, 160
Analyze ways writers organize and present ideas (e.g., comparison-contrast, cause-effect, chronology).	77
Read from and understand the distinguishing features of nonfiction texts (e.g., textbooks, scientific studies, magazines, newspapers).	26, 75, 157
WRITING	
Use conventions of punctuation and capitalization.	1, 4, 5, 9, 10, 17, 18, 19, 20, 33, 33, 60, 64, 68, 78, 80, 83, 84, 87, 88, 89, 90, 95, 96, 97, 98, 101, 102, 103, 104, 128, 129, 130, 131, 132, 133, 134, 135, 136, 138, 140, 141, 142, 143, 144, 145, 146, 147, 148, 149, 150, 151, 152, 153 ,154, 155, 156, 158
Use various parts of speech correctly in writing (e.g., subject-verb agreement, noun and verb forms, objective and subjective case pronouns, correct form of adjectives and adverbs).	2, 3, 4, 5, 6, 7, 8, 9, 10, 11, 12, 13, 14, 15, 22, 27, 28, 29, 31, 32, 33, 34, 37, 41, 42, 43, 44, 45, 46, 47, 48, 49, 52, 53, 54, 55, 60, 61, 62, 63, 64, 65, 66, 68, 69, 70, 72, 73, 77, 78, 79, 80, 83, 84, 87, 92, 94, 95, 96, 99, 100, 107, 108, 109, 112, 121, 122, 128, 136, 137, 140, 144, 154
Write for a variety of occasions, audiences, and purposes (e.g., letters to invite or thank, stories or poems to entertain, information to record, notes and summaries reflecting comprehension).	1, 4, 10, 11, 12, 14, 17, 19, 30, 33, 45, 46, 47, 48, 49, 54, 55, 60, 64, 68, 73, 78, 80, 83, 84, 92, 96, 103, 108, 109, 112, 121, 122, 136, 140, 144, 152, 154
LANGUAGE	
Understand symbols, similes, metaphors, analogies, alliteration, and idiomatic language.	128

Texas Standards Matrix for Grades 5–6

LANGUAGE ARTS STANDARDS	ACTIVITIES
READING	
Apply knowledge of letter-sound correspondences, structural analysis, and context to recognize words and identify root words with affixes.	2, 10, 23, 24, 25, 26, 27, 28, 29, 35, 36, 64, 66, 71, 72, 88, 109, 113, 114, 115, 116, 117, 118, 119, 120, 121, 122, 123, 124, 125, 126, 127, 128
Locate the meanings, pronunciations, and derivations of unfamiliar words using a dictionary, a thesaurus, a glossary, and available technology.	23, 24, 25, 26, 29, 31, 32, 33, 34, 64, 65, 67, 68, 89, 98, 99, 109, 110, 111, 113, 114, 115, 116, 117, 118, 119, 120, 121, 122, 123, 124, 126, 127, 128, 137, 155, 161, 162
Read classic and contemporary works from varied sources, such as plays, anthologies, novels, textbooks, newspapers, and manuals from both print and electronic sources.	26, 75
Follow strategies for comprehension while reading, such as rereading, using reference aids, searching for clues, and asking questions.	3, 8, 11, 12, 14, 16, 18, 20, 21, 22, 26, 35, 36, 39, 40, 41, 42, 43, 44, 53, 54, 55, 56, 57, 58, 59, 61, 62, 63, 65, 66, 69, 70, 73, 75, 81, 82, 85, 86, 91, 94, 95, 99, 100, 101, 102, 105, 106, 146, 147
Answer different types and levels of questions.	15, 20, 35, 39, 40, 56, 81, 82, 105, 106, 125, 146, 159, 160
WRITING	
Write for a variety of audiences and purposes, such as to express, to influence, to inform, to entertain, to record, to problem solve, and to reflect.	1, 4, 5, 6, 10, 17, 19, 30, 33, 45, 46, 47, 48, 49, 54, 55, 60, 64, 68, 73, 78, 80, 83, 84, 87, 92, 96, 109, 112, 121, 122, 128, 136, 140, 141, 142, 144, 154, 158
Compose original texts, applying the conventions of written language, such as capitalization, punctuation, and penmanship, to communicate clearly.	1, 4, 5, 10, 17, 19, 30, 33, 46, 47, 54, 55, 60, 64, 68, 73, 78, 80, 84, 87, 92, 96, 104, 109, 112, 128, 129, 130, 131, 132, 133, 134, 135, 136, 140, 144, 154, 158
Write with accurate spelling of roots, inflections, affixes, and syllable constructions.	1, 4, 5, 11, 12, 14, 17, 19, 27, 28, 29, 31, 32, 33, 34, 35, 37, 46, 47, 60, 64, 66, 78, 80, 83, 84, 87, 95, 97, 98, 104, 121, 122, 128, 136, 140, 144, 152, 154, 158
Use regular and irregular plurals correctly and adjust verbs for agreement.	8, 9, 10, 11, 12, 14, 27, 28, 29, 37
Write in complete sentences, varying the types, such as compound and complex, to match meanings and purposes.	1, 4, 17, 19, 46, 47, 48, 49, 54, 55, 60, 68, 78, 79, 80, 83, 84, 87, 92, 96, 98, 103, 108, 109, 112, 121, 122, 128, 136, 140, 144, 154, 158
Use prepositional phrases, adjectives, and adverbs to make writing vivid and precise.	50, 51, 52, 60, 64, 69, 72, 74, 112, 137

ACTIVITY 1   Define Grammar

Name: _____

Date: _____

Grammar involves learning the rules of how words are joined to form sentences. It includes using the correct words and the correct forms of words. Correct capitalization and punctuation are also part of grammar.

Write what the word *grammar* means to you. _____

_____

_____

_____

Give three reasons why grammar is important for you to learn.

_____

_____

_____

_____

ACTIVITY 2   Identify Common and
Proper Nouns

Name: _____

Date: _____

Nouns are words that name people, places, things, or ideas.
Common nouns do not name specific people, places, or things.
    Examples: hamster, radio, lawyer, and town are common nouns.
Proper nouns name specific people, places, or things.
    Examples: Joa, Lincoln Memorial, and Statue of Liberty are proper nouns.
Always capitalize proper nouns.

Circle all of the nouns. Above each noun, write "C" for common or "P" for proper.

1. Joey plans to visit his grandparents in Sidney, Australia.

2. His grandparents moved there last March.

3. Australia is a continent south of the equator.

4. The poisonous blue-ringed octopus lives in reefs off the coast.

5. Joey hopes to see kangaroos, wombats, bandicoots, dingoes, and maybe even a platypus or Tasmanian devil during his visit.

ACTIVITY 3 Write Common and Proper Nouns

Name:_____

Date:_____

Common nouns do not name specific people, places, or things.

Proper nouns name specific people, places, or things. Always capitalize proper nouns.

1. Write five common nouns that name people. _____ _____

    _____ _____ _____

2. Write five common nouns that name places. _____ _____

    _____ _____ _____

3. Write five common nouns that name things. _____ _____

    _____ _____ _____

4. Write five proper nouns that name people. _____ _____

    _____ _____ _____

5. Write five proper nouns that name places. _____ _____

    _____ _____ _____

6. Write five proper nouns that name things. _____ _____

    _____ _____ _____

- -

ACTIVITY 4 Use Common and Proper Nouns in Context

Name:_____

Date:_____

Write sentences using the words given. Use three or more nouns in each sentence. Underline all of the nouns. Above each noun, write "C" for common or "P" for proper.

1. (hamster) _____

    _____

2. (Greg) _____

    _____

3. (Michigan) _____

    _____

4. (porch) _____

    _____

5. (mayor) _____

    _____

ACTIVITY 5 Identify Concrete and Abstract Nouns

Name:_____

Date:_____

- **Concrete nouns** name people or things that can be seen, heard, tasted, smelled, or touched. *Examples:* porch, porpoise, Peter, and park
- **Abstract nouns** name ideas. They are things you cannot see, hear, taste, smell, or touch. *Examples:* fear, love, friendship, and trust
- A word can be more than one type of noun.
    Jill is both a proper noun and a concrete noun.

Write "C" for concrete or "A" for abstract to label each noun.

1.	_____ dedication	5.	_____ aroma	9.	_____ shoelace
2.	_____ door	6.	_____ crash	10.	_____ Alaska
3.	_____ honesty	7.	_____ quarter	11.	_____ pride
4.	_____ dishonesty	8.	_____ curiosity	12.	_____ intelligence

Write a sentence using two abstract nouns not listed above.

_____

_____

ACTIVITY 6 Classify Nouns

Name:_____

Date:_____

Write the nouns from the list in the correct sections. All words fit in more than one category.

Cecelia   ceiling   chills   people   pins   poverty
property   terror   Terry   Tuesday   turtles   wand
weather   William   wisdom   wizard   world   worries

Common	Proper	Concrete	Abstract

ACTIVITY 7 Identify Active Verbs

Name:_____

Date:_____

A **verb** is a word that tells what something does or that something exists.
Active verbs tell what nouns (people, places, or things) do, did, or will do.
   Examples: hop, skip, and jump
A sentence can contain more than one verb and/or more than one noun.

Underline the nouns that tell who or what did something and write them in the "Who or What" column. Circle the verbs. Write the verbs in the "Did What" column.

	Who or What	Did What
1. My cousin found a large snake.	_____	_____
2. The snake shed its skin.	_____	_____
3. Not all snakes hatch from eggs.	_____	_____
4. Kay wrote and directed the play.	_____	_____
5. The audience stood and clapped.	_____	_____
6. Everyone enjoyed the play.	_____	_____
7. Wendy watched the walrus waddle.	_____	_____
8. Did Joe hit a home run?	_____	_____
9. Why can't ostriches fly?	_____	_____

ACTIVITY 8 Write Present Tense of Active Verbs

Name:_____

Date:_____

Verb tense tells when an event happens, happened, or will happen. Verb tense tells when someone does, did, or will do something. **Present tense** means something happens now or someone does something now.
   Examples: Shirley sings.   Herman hums.

Write a present tense, active verb to complete each sentence.

1. Fred _____ flat tires.

2. Greg _____ flowers.

3. You _____ home after school.

4. Our teacher _____ us too much homework.

5. Mort _____ very often.

6. Patti _____ the piano.

7. The cat _____ the tree.

8. The dragon _____ fire.

ACTIVITY 9   Write Future Tense of Verbs   Name:_____

Date:_____

Future tense indicates something will happen or someone will do something later.
Examples: I shall find your glasses. Will you put them in a safe place?

Form the future tense of verbs by combining a present tense verb with *will* or *shall*. Change the verb to future tense and rewrite each sentence.

1. I go to New York.

_____

2. They sing in the chorus.

_____

3. I take my hamster for a walk.

_____

4. The engineers fixed the problem.

_____

5. Flowers grew in my garden.

_____

_____

ACTIVITY 10   Write Past Tense of   Name:_____
Regular Verbs
Date:_____

Past tense indicates something happened or someone did something before now. To write the past tense of regular verbs, add *-ed* to the end of the word.
Examples: connect – connected   add – added   frown – frowned
If the verb ends in an *e*, drop the *e*, and add *-ed*.
Examples: hike – hiked   love – loved   smile – smiled

Write sentences on another sheet of paper using the past tense of the verbs listed.

1. enjoy   5. move

2. walk   6. rain

3. wiggle   7. laugh

4. watch   8. tickle

ACTIVITY 11   Use Inactive Verbs in Context

Name: _____

Date: _____

Inactive verbs express a state of being. Forms of the verb *to be* (*is, am, are, was, were, be,* and *been*) are the most common inactive verbs.

> *Examples:* Fred <u>is</u> late today.
>
> Fred <u>was</u> late yesterday.
>
> <u>Will</u> Fred <u>be</u> on time tomorrow?

Write an inactive verb to complete each sentence.

1. Max and Connie _____ my cousins.
2. Connie _____ older than me.
3. Max _____ adopted.
4. I _____ younger than Max.
5. I _____ at the lake by 8:30 to meet Max and Connie.
6. We _____ at the lake last Saturday.
7. They _____ happy.
8. Max _____ shorter than Connie.
9. We have _____ at the lake many times.
10. Have you _____ to the lake lately?

ACTIVITY 12   Use Linking Verbs in Context

Name: _____

Date: _____

Inactive verbs are often used as linking verbs.

> *Examples:* Fred and Fern <u>are running</u> late again.
>
> Fred <u>was running</u> late yesterday.
>
> Fern <u>will</u> probably <u>be running</u> late again tomorrow.

Write a linking verb with an active verb to complete each sentence.

1. The worms _____ in the garden.
2. The whale _____ in the ocean.
3. In the sky, clouds _____ .
4. We _____ for the rain.
5. The sky _____ darker.
6. The ants _____ home before the rain begins.
7. My aunts _____ a big party.
8. My uncles _____ fishing.

ACTIVITY 13 Use Inactive Verbs in Context

Name:_____

Date:_____

Inactive verbs express a state of being. Inactive verbs can be singular or plural (is/are). They can be present, past, or future tense (am/was/will be). Some verbs like *feel, sound, taste, look, appear, grow, seem,* and *smell* can be active or inactive. Inactive verbs are often followed by an adjective that describes the subject of the sentence. *Examples:* I feel happy today.

Underline the inactive verb in each sentence.

1. The trees look taller each year.
2. The band seemed ready to begin the concert.
3. The audience appeared tired of waiting.
4. The concert sounded too loud.
5. Do the fresh tomatoes taste good?
6. Norma felt cold.
7. The cookies smelled delicious.
8. José looked happy about his grades.

ACTIVITY 14 Identify Inactive Verbs/ Write Sentences

Name:_____

Date:_____

Inactive verbs are usually followed by a word or words that tell more about the subject of the sentence. *Examples:*   Glenda *looks* <u>hungry</u>.
    Charlene *felt* <u>frightened</u> and <u>lonely</u>.
    Dora *is* my <u>sister</u>.
Inactive verbs are often followed by an adjective that describes the subject of the sentence.
    Example: I *felt* <u>sick</u> while we were on the boat. (inactive)
Active verbs are often followed by a noun.
    Example: I *felt* the <u>wind</u> in my hair while we sailed. (active)

Write an adjective after the inactive verb that tells more about the subject.
1. Does Angie feel _____?
2. The storm sounded _____.
3. Does the pie taste _____?
4. You seem _____.
5. Do the melons smell _____?
6. Did the dragon look _____?
7. The knight was _____.
8. The hamsters were _____.
9. Uncle Joe's whiskers felt _____.

ACTIVITY 15 Review Active and Inactive Verbs

Name:_____

Date:_____

Underline the verbs. Write "A" for active verb or "I" for inactive verb.

1. _____ Jody felt the cold rain on her head.
2. _____ Jody felt cold in the rain.
3. _____ Joe sounded the alarm.
4. _____ Joe sounded tired.
5. _____ The dish ran away with the spoon.
6. _____ Blossoms grow on fruit trees.
7. _____ Sarah grew impatient with her brother.
8. _____ Your flute solo sounded fantastic.
9. _____ A large shadow appeared on the window.
10. _____ The shadow seemed scary to Brenda.
11. _____ Brad smelled the skunk.
12. _____ The skunk smelled terrible.

ACTIVITY 16 Identify Sentences and Sentence Fragments

Name:_____

Date:_____

- A **sentence** is a word or group of words that expresses a complete thought.   *Example:* Nancy dances.
- Always **capitalize** the first word of a sentence.
- A **fragment** is a group of words that <u>does not</u> express a complete thought.   *Example:* Before sunrise

Write "Y" for yes or "N" for no to show if each group of words is a sentence. Add a period to the words that are complete sentences.

1. _____ Tina ran away
2. _____ Jake juggled
3. _____ Only in July
4. _____ So much alike
5. _____ Snakes slither
6. _____ Alone, after dark
7. _____ Far from the ocean

8. _____ Walking to school
9. _____ Sally hops
10. _____ Did the hamster
11. _____ Across the lake on skis
12. _____ Seashells on the beach
13. _____ Winning isn't everything
14. _____ When the leaves fell

ACTIVITY 17 **Write Declarative and Imperative Sentences**

Name:_____

Date:_____

A **declarative sentence** states a fact or provides information. A declarative sentence ends with a period.

> *Examples:*   Venus is often called the morning star.
> Pedro prepared pizza for Paco.

Write a declarative sentence on another sheet of paper for each pair of words.

1. (dinosaurs, roamed)
2. (baseball, play)
3. (spotted lizards)

Imperative sentences are commands. They tell someone what to do. Imperative sentences end with a period.

> *Examples:*   Brush your teeth after you eat.
> You must finish your homework before you leave.

Write an imperative sentence on another sheet of paper for each pair of words.

4. (you, wash)   5. (climb, carefully)   6. (watch, baby)

ACTIVITY 18 **Identify Exclamatory Sentences**

Name:_____

Date:_____

Exclamatory sentences show surprise or strong feelings. They are usually short and always end with an exclamation point.   *Examples:* Stop right now!   Watch out!

Add the correct punctuation at the end of each sentence.

1. Stay back
2. Save your money
3. Stop
4. Do it right now
5. Help

6. Watch out for that skunk
7. Don't touch
8. Call an ambulance
9. Come right now
10. The fog is getting thicker

ACTIVITY 19 **Write Interrogative Sentences**

Name: _____

Date: _____

Interrogative sentences ask questions. An interrogative sentence ends with a **question mark**.
Examples: Can you lift this piano?   How did you get so strong?

Write interrogative sentences that include the words listed. Use a question mark at the end of the sentences.

1. will _____

   _____

2. would _____

   _____

3. should _____

   _____

4. could _____

   _____

5. might _____

   _____

- -

ACTIVITY 20 **Review End of Sentence Punctuation**

Name: _____

Date: _____

Add the correct punctuation at the end of each sentence.
1. Did your puppy learn any new tricks
2. What a great trick
3. How did he do that
4. You should train your puppy not to bark so much
5. Stop barking
6. Many people prefer dogs rather than cats as pets

Circle "T" for true or "F" for false.
7. T   F   A fragment does not express a complete thought.
8. T   F   Interrogative sentences end in an exclamation point.
9. T   F   A sentence can be one word long.
10. T   F   Some sentences do not need any punctuation at the end.
11. T   F   An imperative sentence ends with a question mark.
12. T   F   A declarative sentence states a fact.

Write an imperative sentence. _____

_____

ACTIVITY 21 Identify Subjects and Predicates

Name:_____

Date:_____

The **subject** of a sentence names who or what the sentence is about. The subject of a sentence includes a noun or pronoun and all related words. The subject can be one word or more than one word.

The **predicate** of a sentence tells what the subject does, is, or has. The predicate of a sentence includes a verb and all related words. The predicate can be one word or more than one word.

Examples: We   /   saw many beautiful birds at the aviary.
      (subject) /   (predicate)
      All the king's horses and all the king's men   /   ran away.
      (subject)   /   (predicate)

Underline the subjects. Circle the predicates.

1. Carla painted the bedroom, kitchen, and bathroom.
2. After he slept for nine hours, Jason felt much better.
3. After lunch, Tori and Emily went swimming.
4. My grandmother wore a large straw hat in the garden.
5. Silver bells and cockle shells grow in Mary's garden.
6. Can a hamster learn to do tricks?

ACTIVITY 22 Write Subjects and Predicates

Name:_____

Date:_____

The **subject** of a sentence names who or what the sentence is about. A subject can be one word or more than one word. If there is no subject given, the subject is *you.*

Examples: Come here.   Stop that!

Write a subject to complete each sentence.

1. _____ arrived late again.
2. Will _____ be ready before noon?
3. _____ missed her plane.
4. Did _____ remember your birthday?

The **predicate** of a sentence tells what the subject does, is, or has. In interrogative sentences, the words in the predicate can be separated by the subject. A predicate can be one word or more than one word.

Write a predicate to complete each sentence.

5. Our coach _____.
6. The dentist _____.
7. _____ you and _____?
8. _____ the hamster _____?

ACTIVITY 23 Add "s" or "es" to Write Plural Nouns

Name:_____

Date:_____

- **Singular** means *one*.
  Skunk, brother, dream, and *night* are singular nouns.

- **Plural** means *more than one*.
  Skunks, brothers, dreams, and *nights* are plural nouns.

To write the plural of most nouns, add *s* to the end of the word.

Write the plural for each noun.

1. star _____
2. step _____
3. seagull _____
4. sparrow _____

5. sun _____
6. son _____
7. sound _____
8. shirt _____

- When a singular noun ends in *s, x,* or *z,* you usually add *es* to write the plural.
  Examples: bass/basses   fox/foxes
- When a singular noun ends in *ch* or *sh,* add *es* to write the plural.
  Examples: ash/ashes   watch/watches

Write the plural for each noun. Use a dictionary if you need help.

9. wish _____
10. fuss _____
11. dish _____
12. brush _____

13. arch _____
14. bench _____
15. tax _____
16. grass _____

ACTIVITY 24 Write Plurals of Nouns Ending in "y"

Name:_____

Date:_____

When a noun ends in *y,* usually add *s* to write the plural if a vowel comes before the *y.*
   Examples: jay – jays   day – days   boy – boys

When a noun ends in *y,* usually change the *y* to *i* and add *es* to write the plural if a consonant comes before the *y.*
   Examples: try – tries   butterfly – butterflies   spy – spies

Write the plural for each word. Use a dictionary if you need help.

1. canary _____
2. buddy _____
3. fly _____
4. story _____
5. delay _____
6. array _____
7. Tuesday _____
8. guppy _____

9. way _____
10. pony _____
11. lady _____
12. toy _____
13. cry _____
14. dandy _____
15. fry _____
16. dye _____

ACTIVITY 25   Write Plurals of Irregular Nouns

Name:_____

Date:_____

The singular and plural of some nouns are spelled the same.

    Examples: moose   sheep   pajamas

The spelling of the plurals of some nouns changes completely.

    Examples: hoof – hooves   goose – geese

Write the plurals for these nouns. Use a dictionary if you need help.

1. life _____
2. hero _____
3. mouse _____
4. scarf _____
5. cattle _____
6. scissors _____
7. person _____
8. potato _____

9. tooth _____
10. jeans _____
11. elf _____
12. deer _____
13. ox _____
14. leaf _____
15. knife _____
16. loaf _____

ACTIVITY 26   Write Singular and Plural Nouns

Name:_____

Date:_____

Make a copy of a newspaper or magazine article. Underline all of the common nouns. Write singular nouns in the singular column and plural nouns in the plural column. If a noun appears more than once, list it only once. Then write the missing singular or plural form for each noun. Use another sheet of paper if you need more room. Use a dictionary if you need help.

Singular	Plural	Singular	Plural
_____	_____	_____	_____
_____	_____	_____	_____
_____	_____	_____	_____
_____	_____	_____	_____
_____	_____	_____	_____
_____	_____	_____	_____
_____	_____	_____	_____
_____	_____	_____	_____

ACTIVITY 27 Write Singular and Plural Verbs

Name:_____

Date:_____

Like nouns, verbs can be singular or plural. Unlike nouns, verbs that end in an *s* are usually singular.   *Examples:*

Singular	**Plural**
Angie runs.	Angie and Joe run.
The hamster squeaks.	Hamsters squeak.
The boat sails.	Boats sail.

Write the missing form of each underlined verb.

Singular

1. Sara <u>sighs</u>.
2. Maya _____.
3. Bill _____.
4. A lion <u>roars</u>.
5. A flower <u>grows</u>.
6. A leaf _____.
7. Ann <u>answers</u>.

Plural

Sara and Sue _____.

Maya and Don <u>wish</u>.

Bill and Ben <u>run</u>.

Lions _____.

Flowers _____.

Leaves <u>fall</u>.

They _____.

ACTIVITY 28 Identify Singular and Plural Nouns/Write Verbs

Name:_____

Date:_____

Use a **singular** verb with a **singular** subject. Use a **plural** verb with a **plural** subject.

Underline the nouns that are the subjects of the sentences. Write "S" for singular or "P" for plural. Write a singular or plural, present tense verb to complete each sentence.

1. _____ The band _____ great.
2. _____ The audience _____ the play.
3. _____ The children _____ apples in fall.
4. _____ A journey of 1,000 miles _____ with the first step.
5. _____ If it rains, the roof _____.
6. _____ My brothers and I _____ to build snowmen in winter.
7. _____ The rusty old door _____ when we open it.
8. _____ The ducks on my grandfather's farm _____ in a pond.
9. _____ During the monsoon season, it _____ often.
10. _____ My brother always _____ to close the back door.

ACTIVITY 29 Write Singular and Plural Verbs

Name: _____

Date: _____

The spelling guidelines for verbs are similar to those for nouns. Usually, *es* is added if the word ends in *s, x, z, ch,* or *sh*. Review the rules for words that end in *y*.

Write the singular present tense form for each verb. Use a dictionary if you need help.

1. We try to find our way home.   He _____ to find his way home.

2. We wish for fish.   Trish _____ for fish.

3. Cats chase mice.   A cat _____ mice.

4. Mosquitoes buzz.   A mosquito _____.

5. We wax our skis every week.   Sheila _____ her skis every week.

6. They fish for trout.   Greg _____ for trout.

7. They pass the salt.   Sal _____ the salt.

8. We say, "Hello."   She _____, "Hello."

9. They box the books.   Jessie _____ the books.

10. Birds hatch from eggs.   A bird _____ from an egg.

ACTIVITY 30 Critical Thinking

Name: _____

Date: _____

When verbs are used in the past tense, does the spelling change for singular and plural? Give several examples to support your answer.

_____

_____

_____

_____

When verbs are used in the future tense, does the spelling change for singular and plural? Give several examples to support your answer.

_____

_____

_____

_____

15

ACTIVITY 31 Write Past Tense of Irregular Verbs

Name:_____

Date:_____

Some verbs are **irregular**. The past tense is not formed by dropping the *e* and adding *ed*.
  Examples: write – wrote   think – thought   do – did

Fill in the irregular verb chart. Use a dictionary if you need help.

Present Tense	Past Tense		Present Tense	Past Tense
1. bend	_____	11. _____		said
2. bind	_____	12. send		_____
3. _____	bought	13. shake		_____
4. _____	caught	14. _____		ate
5. bite	_____	15. tear		_____
6. blow	_____	16. tell		_____
7. _____	broke	17. _____		fed
8. build	_____	18. _____		fought
9. _____	dug	19. _____		found
10. _____	dealt	20. wear		_____

ACTIVITY 32 Write Past Tense of Irregular Verbs

Name:_____

Date:_____

Some verbs are **irregular**. The past tense is not formed by dropping the *e* and adding *ed*.
  Examples: write – wrote   think – thought   do – did

Fill in the irregular verb chart. Use a dictionary if you need help.

Present Tense	Past Tense		Present Tense	Past Tense
1. fling	_____	11. sweep		_____
2. forget	_____	12. swing		_____
3. _____	forgave	13. mean		_____
4. _____	fell	14. _____		sat
5. go	_____	15. _____		rang
6. grow	_____	16. spend		_____
7. _____	had	17. _____		arose
8. keep	_____	18. _____		awoke
9. _____	led	19. _____		became
10. _____	left	20. speak		_____

ACTIVITY 33 Use Irregular Verbs in Context/Write Sentences

Name:_____

Date:_____

The **past tense** of some irregular verbs, such as *quit, set,* and *shut* are spelled the same in present and past tense.

Write a short sentence using the past tense of each verb. Check a dictionary if you are unsure of the spelling.

1. bet _____
2 blow _____
3. burn _____
4. cast _____
5. catch _____
6. cost _____
7. cut _____
8. let _____
9. put _____

- -

ACTIVITY 34 Write Past Participles of Verbs

Name:_____

Date:_____

- The **past participle** form of a verb is formed by using *has, had,* or *have* with a verb.
- The spelling of the past participle of regular verbs is the same as the simple past tense.
    Examples: have raced   had fished   have giggled   has hiked
- The spelling of the past participle of irregular verbs can be different than the simple past tense.   *Examples:*   have flown   had run   have sung   has forgotten

Write the past and past participle forms for these verbs. Use a dictionary if you are unsure of the spelling.

Present	Past	Past Participle	
1. drink	_____	has, have, or had	_____
2. think	_____	has, have, or had	_____
3. know	_____	has, have, or had	_____
4. wear	_____	has, have, or had	_____
5. cut	_____	has, have, or had	_____
6. bring	_____	has, have, or had	_____
7. swim	_____	has, have, or had	_____

ACTIVITY 35 Review Verb Tense

Name:_____

Date:_____

Write the word that matches the description.

1. _____ Present tense, singular of *spent*
2. _____ Future tense of *rise*
3. _____ Past participle of *catch*
4. _____ Future tense of *set*
5. _____ Present tense, plural of *keep*
6. _____ Present tense, singular of *meant*
7. _____ Past participle of *put*
8. _____ Past tense of *build*
9. _____ Future tense of *rid*
10. _____ Past tense of *cut*
11. _____ Present tense, singular of *fed*
12. _____ Past participle of *mow*
13. _____ Future tense of *swing*
14. _____ Present tense, plural, of *bought*
15. _____ Future tense of *sank*
16. _____ Past participle of *grow*

ACTIVITY 36 Review Verb Forms

Name:_____

Date:_____

Underline the verbs. Circle present, past participle, or future to match the verb form.

1. Josh will go to the zoo on Saturday.	Present	Past Participle	Future
2. He enjoys the penguins.	Present	Past Participle	Future
3. They had moved to Maine last year.	Present	Past Participle	Future
4. Do you like to ski?	Present	Past Participle	Future
5. I prefer skating and sledding.	Present	Past Participle	Future
6. We had visited them in December.	Present	Past Participle	Future
7. We go to the zoo once a month.	Present	Past Participle	Future
8. Darla's father works at the zoo.	Present	Past Participle	Future

Write sentences using the verb forms given.

9. *giggle*, future tense _____

_____

10. *chuckle*, past tense _____

_____

11. *swell*, past participle _____

_____

ACTIVITY 37 Identify Collective Nouns   Name:_____

Date:_____

* **Collective nouns** name groups composed of members.
    Examples: audience   flock   class   group
* **Collective nouns** are singular. Use a singular verb with a collective noun.
    Examples: The audience waits for the play to begin.   The class is restless today.

Finish the sentences using these collective nouns. Be sure to use singular verbs.

1. The troop _____

2. Our team _____

3. A society _____

4. The jury _____

5. My family _____

6. That committee _____

7. The farmer's herd _____

ACTIVITY 38 Review Types of Nouns   Name:_____

Date:_____

Label each noun as *common, proper, concrete, abstract,* and/or *collective.* All nouns fit into more than one category.

1. _____ Brooklyn Bridge

2. _____ lake

3. _____ love

4. _____ shore

5. _____ herd

6. _____ compassion

7. _____ reputation

8. _____ Matt

9. _____ staff

10. _____ doctor

11. _____ Hancock Building

12. _____ Ms. Johnson

13. _____ Germany

ACTIVITY 39   Review Terms/Test-Taking

Name:_____

Date:_____

Match the terms with their definitions.

1. _____ future tense verb
2. _____ irregular verbs
3. _____ abstract noun
4. _____ past tense verb
5. _____ plural
6. _____ predicate
7. _____ present tense verb

8. _____ proper noun
9. _____ inactive verb
10. _____ sentence
11. _____ subject
12. _____ concrete nouns

13. _____ past participle

14. _____ collective nouns

a. names who or what a sentence is about
b. words that name groups composed of members
c. the form of a verb combined with *have* or *had*
d. a word that names a specific person, place, or thing
e. a word that expresses a state of being
f. a word that shows something is happening now
g. words that name people or things that can be seen, heard, tasted, smelled, or touched
h. a word that shows something will happen later
i. verbs that do not end in -*ed* in the past tense
j. a word that shows something happened before now
k. more than one
l. a word or group of words that expresses a complete thought
m. words that name things that cannot be seen, heard, tasted, smelled, or touched
n. word or words in a sentence that tells what the subject does, is, or has

ACTIVITY 40   Review/Test-Taking

Name:_____

Date:_____

Circle "T" for true or "F" for false.

1. T   F   A declarative sentence ends with a period.

2. T   F   A declarative sentence states a fact or gives a command.

3. T   F   A fragment is a group of words that does not express a complete thought.

4. T   F   Abstract nouns are things that cannot be seen, heard, tasted, smelled, or touched.

5. T   F   Always use a singular verb with a singular subject.

6. T   F   If a verb ends in an *s*, it is probably plural.

7. T   F   Imperative sentences end with an exclamation point.

8. T   F   Never capitalize common nouns.

9. T   F   Sentences that show surprise or strong feelings end with a question mark.

10. T   F   The subject of a sentence can be more than one word.

11. T   F   Use a singular verb with collective nouns.

12. T   F   Verbs tell what nouns do.

ACTIVITY 41 Identify Subjective Pronouns and Their Antecedents

Name:_____

Date:_____

Pronouns are often used in place of nouns to avoid repetition. Pronouns can name people, places, things, or ideas. The nouns to which pronouns refer are called their **antecedents**. The word *antecedent* means "going before."

Subjective pronouns take the place of nouns as subjects of sentences. They refer to people or things.   **Singular:**   I   you   he   she   it
Plural: we   you   they

If a noun is **singular**, use a <u>singular</u> pronoun to replace it. If the noun is **plural**, use a <u>plural</u> pronoun. If a singular noun is **masculine** or **feminine**, use a <u>masculine</u> or <u>feminine</u> pronoun. Otherwise, use *it*.

Underline the subjective pronouns. Write the word or words the pronouns replace.

1. My name is Ishmael; I am a sailor.   _____
2. Captain Ahab was our captain. We feared him.   _____
3. He pursued Moby Dick, a great white whale.   _____
4. He wanted revenge for the loss of his leg.   _____
5. When the storm rolled in, it was scary.   _____
6. The crew and I could not reason with Captain Ahab.   _____
7. We wanted to give up the chase.   _____
8. Have you ever sailed on a large ship in a storm?   _____

ACTIVITY 42 Write Nouns for Subjective Pronouns

Name:_____

Date:_____

- One pronoun can replace two or more nouns.

    Example: <u>Holly</u>, <u>Molly</u>, and <u>Polly</u> are triplets.   <u>They</u> are triplets.

- Use a singular pronoun with a singular verb and a plural pronoun with a plural verb.

    Exceptions: The pronouns *I* and *you* use a <u>plural</u> verb.

    Examples: I jog daily.   I lift weights.   You eat spinach.

What do you notice about the pronoun *you*?_____
_____

Underline the subjective pronouns. Write nouns to replace the pronouns.

1. He and I had a good time camping.   _____
2. We spent a week at Yellowstone National Park.   _____
3. We will go to a museum tomorrow.   _____
4. They will take us on a tour.   _____
5. It will take two hours.   _____
6. It features a huge Egyptian exhibit.   _____
7. He will show us a movie about King Tut.   _____
8. You can come, too.   _____

ACTIVITY 43 Identify Adjectives and the Nouns They Describe

Name:_____

Date:_____

- **Adjectives** are words that tell more about nouns or pronouns.
- Adjectives describe the size, shape, color, or number of someone or something.
  Examples: smelly   seven   silly   short
- The same adjective can describe more than one noun in a sentence.
- More than one adjective can describe one noun.

Underline all of the adjectives. Draw arrows to the nouns they describe. Do not underline *a*, *an*, or *the*.
  Example: Karla threw the <u>colorful beach</u> ball to the <u>playful brown</u> dog.

1. The purple finch laid three small eggs in her nest in the tall maple tree.

2. She used wrapping paper decorated with yellow, blue, and green swirls and big red dots.

3. The new coach really liked the green carpeting with the gold and white team logos.

4. A huge oak desk and bookcase filled the small office.

5. We ate cheese, pepperoni, onion, and mushroom pizza and garlic breadsticks.

ACTIVITY 44 Identify Adjectives and the Nouns They Describe

Name:_____

Date:_____

Sometimes adjectives are separated from the nouns they describe by other words.

  Example: Juan enjoyed the <u>hot spicy</u> peppers.

  The peppers were <u>hot</u> and <u>spicy</u>.

Underline all adjectives. Draw arrows to the nouns they describe.

1. All insects have a hard exoskeleton, a three-part body, three pairs of jointed legs, compound eyes, and two antennae.

2. There are about a million different types of insects.

3. The largest insect ever was the ancient dragonfly called Meganeura.

4. This predatory flying insect lived in prehistoric times and had a two-foot wingspan.

5. Male crickets make a loud chirping sound by rubbing their forewings together.

6. A praying mantis catches its prey with its strong, barbed front legs.

7. Which insect do you think is the most interesting?

22

ACTIVITY 45 Write Adjectives to Describe Nouns

Name:_____

Date:_____

Adjectives are words that describe nouns or pronouns. Separate three or more adjectives in a row with commas, even when the word *and* is not used.

Write three or more adjectives to describe each noun. Use commas to separate the adjectives.
  Example: *large, blue, yellow,* and *green* butterfly

1. _____ hamster
2. _____ snow
3. _____ donuts
4. _____ tree
5. _____ garden
6. _____ jungle
7. _____ athlete
8. _____ student

ACTIVITY 46 Identify Adjectives/ Write a Tongue Twister

Name:_____

Date:_____

Circle all of the adjectives in these tongue twisters.

1. Brad bought blue brick blocks to build a broad, blue, brick bridge.
2. Shy Sheila sang seven silly songs on a sunny Sunday in September.
3. Cheerful Charlotte chose cherry shakes and chocolates for Charles.
4. Carrie carried caffeine coffee in a copper coffee cup.
5. Big Billy, the Boston bully, broke Benny's best bugle. Benny bought a better bugle to blast Big Billy back to Boston.
6. Chet chewed the chewy cheddar cheese chunks Charlie chose.

Write two tongue twisters that include three or more adjectives. Underline the adjectives.

_____

_____

_____

_____

On another sheet of paper, write one or more adjectives for every letter of the alphabet except *x*.

ACTIVITY 47 Use Adjectives in Context/ Write Sentences

Name:_____

Date:_____

Adjectives are words that tell more about nouns or pronouns. They describe the size, shape, color, or number of someone or something.

Example: We found <u>three</u>, <u>large</u>, <u>green</u> and <u>yellow</u>, <u>square</u> presents in the closet.

Size = <u>large</u> *Shape* = <u>square</u>   *Color* = <u>green, yellow</u> *Number* = <u>three</u>

Write sentences using adjectives to describe each item.

1. The size, shape, and color of storm clouds _____

   _____

2. The number, shapes, and sizes of any items in a kitchen _____

   _____

3. The color, size, and number of flowers in a garden _____

   _____

4. The size, shape, and number of amps at a concert _____

   _____

5. Describe a character from a novel. _____

   _____

ACTIVITY 48 Differentiate Between Adjectives and Nouns/Write Sentences

Name:_____

Date:_____

Some words have more than one meaning and can be used as more than one part of speech. *Examples:*   **Peas** are my favorite vegetable. (a noun)

I enjoy **pea** soup for lunch. (an adjective that describes the soup)

Write "N" if the boldface word is a noun. Write "A" if it is an adjective. Use clues from the sentences to learn what the words mean and how they are used.

1. _____ A cool **spring** morning is a great time to go fishing.
2. _____ Have you ever visited an **art** museum?
3. _____ Do you like **spring** better than autumn?
4. _____ Will you wear your **orange** hat on Halloween?
5. _____ I need a new **watch**; mine broke.
6. _____ When the **spring** broke, the gears flew all over.
7. _____ Would you like an **orange** with your lunch?
8. _____ I need a new **watch** battery.
9. On another sheet of paper, write a sentence using *arch* as a noun.
10. On another sheet of paper, write a sentence using *arch* as an adjective.

24

ACTIVITY 49 Identify Prepositions/ Write Sentences

Name:_____

Date:_____

A **preposition** is a word that comes before a noun or pronoun and introduces a phrase.

These words can be used as prepositions:

about	above	across	after	around	at	before	behind	by
down	for	from	in	into	near	of	off	on
out	over	past	through	to	under	up	without	with

Circle the prepositions.

1. "Over the Rainbow" was a song in the movie, *The Wizard of Oz.*
2. Dorothy traveled with her friends down the yellow brick road, across the field, and through the forest to Oz.
3. The Scarecrow's head was filled with straw.
4. The Cowardly Lion asked the Wizard for courage.
5. A heart was requested by the Tin Man.
6. Dorothy wished she could return to her home and family in Kansas.

On another sheet of paper, write two sentences that include prepositions. Underline them.

ACTIVITY 50 Identify Prepositional Phrases

Name:_____

Date:_____

A **phrase** is a group of words that go together. When a phrase begins with a preposition, it is **a prepositional phrase**.

Examples: around the corner   under the sink   below the water

All prepositional phrases must begin with a preposition and include at least one noun or pronoun. More than one noun or pronoun can be part of a prepositional phrase.

Example: Harry received gifts <u>from Hermione, Ron, and Hagrid</u>.

Underline all prepositional phrases. Circle the nouns and pronouns in each prepositional phrase.

1. The three kittens left their mittens in the house under the rug by the red chair.
2. From the hot air balloon, we looked down at the buildings and across the city to the river.
3. The children followed the piper from the town, across the river, up the mountain, and into an opening in a cave.
4. While on vacation, we took pictures with our camera of the mountains across the valley.
5. Without a doubt, your painting of the rainbow is the best on exhibit.
6. This gift is from me to you for your birthday.
7. The panther ran through the jungle, across the stream, and over the rocky plain to its home territory.

ACTIVITY 51   Differentiate Between
Prepositional and Verb Phrases

Name:_____

Date:_____

All prepositional phrases must begin with a preposition and include at least one noun or pronoun.

> *Example:* **Prepositional phrase:** <u>above the spider web</u> – begins with a preposition and includes a noun.
>
> **Not a prepositional phrase:** <u>to weave quickly</u> – begins with a word that can be a preposition, but does not include a noun or pronoun.

Underline only the prepositional phrases. Circle the numbers of the sentences that do not contain prepositional phrases.

1. He forgot to set the alarm clock.

2. Andy stood behind Amos.

3. Andy was not first in line.

4. Is she near?

5. Would you like to go swimming?

6. Look out!

7. Will you give the book to him?

8. Are you through eating?

9. The students were glad summer vacation was over.

10. Emma stood up too quickly and became dizzy.

- -

ACTIVITY 52   Complete Prepositional
Phrases

Name:_____

Date:_____

Write prepositions to complete the prepositional phrases.

1. _____ the jungle

2. _____ the window

3. _____ you and me

4. _____ his uncle

5. _____ a pond

6. _____ my school

7. _____ a pencil

8. _____ the cornfield

9. _____ the last century

10. _____ Jupiter

11. _____ my hamster

12. _____ a large rock

Finish the prepositional phrases.

13. below _____

14. from _____

15. through _____

16. after _____

17. without _____

18. past _____

19. across _____

20. behind _____

ACTIVITY 53 Use Objective Pronouns in Context

Name:_____

Date:_____

The **object of a prepositional phrase** is the noun or pronoun that follows a preposition and is part of the prepositional phrase. Use only objective pronouns as the objects of prepositional phrases.

Objective pronouns are: **Singular:** me   you   him   her   it

Plural: us   you   them

Two or more pronouns can be the objects of the same preposition.

Example: Uncle Tim bought presents for <u>him</u>, <u>her</u>, <u>me</u>, and <u>them</u>.

Write objective pronouns from the list to complete the sentences.

1. Bonnie has a new puppy. The puppy belongs to _____.
2. Bonnie bought the puppy from Mona and Jerry. She bought the puppy from _____.
3. I brought a toy for the puppy. The toy was brought by _____
4. You will like the puppy. It will appeal to _____.
5. Bonnie and I will train the puppy. It will be trained by _____.
6. You and Andy can visit tomorrow. We'll expect a visit from _____ then.
7. Bonnie and I gave the puppy a bath. The bath was given by Bonnie and _____.

ACTIVITY 54 Use Objective Pronouns/ Write Sentences

Name:_____

Date:_____

Write objective pronouns to complete the sentences.

1. The gift was for _____ and _____.
2. My aunt explained the new computer to _____ and _____.
3. Annette received gifts from _____ and _____.
4. The gifts were for _____ from _____.
5. Amos borrowed a book from _____, but he forgot to give it back to _____.
6. He wouldn't move, so we walked around _____.
7. Will you go to the party with _____ and _____?
8. Anna was first in line, and Gary stood behind _____.

Write two sentences that use objective pronouns.

_____
_____
_____
_____

27

ACTIVITY 55 Review Prepositional Phrases/Interpret Proverbs

Name:_____

Date:_____

A **prepositional phrase** includes the preposition, the object of the preposition, and all related words. **Proverbs** are sayings that offer good advice or words of wisdom.

Underline the prepositional phrases in these proverbs. In your own words, write what you think each one means. If you are unsure, ask someone for help.

1. In for a penny, in for a pound _____

_____

2. Six of one, half a dozen of the other _____

_____

3. Don't cross your bridges before you come to them. _____

_____

4. A stitch in time saves nine. _____

_____

ACTIVITY 56 Review Adjectives, Prepositions, and Pronouns/Test-Taking

Name:_____

Date:_____

Circle "T" for true or "F" for false.

1. T F A prepositional phrase always includes a noun or a pronoun.
2. T F Adjectives are words that describe nouns or pronouns.
3. T F Adjectives describe the size, shape, color, or number of someone or something.
4. T F Adjectives do not describe verbs.
5. T F *Elegant, personal, loud,* and *stormy* are adjectives.
6. T F If a word is an adjective, it can never be used as any other part of speech.
7. T F More than one adjective can describe one noun.
8. T F One adjective can describe more than one noun.
9. T F Separate three or more adjectives in a row with commas.
10. T F Sometimes adjectives come after the word or words they describe.
11. T F *I, he,* and *she* can be used as the objects of a prepositional phrase.
12. T F *Through, near,* and *up* can only be used as prepositions.
13. T F *To hop, to skip,* and *to jump* are prepositional phrases.
14. T F *Too, thorough,* and *lovely* are prepositions.
15. T F *You* and *it* can be used as subjective or objective pronouns.

ACTIVITY 57 Recognize Direct Objects

Name:_____

Date:_____

Direct objects are nouns or pronouns that come after an active verb to complete its meaning. A direct object answers the question *who* or *what*. Use objective pronouns as direct objects. A sentence may have more than one direct object.

Examples: Aaron sent an <u>e-mail</u>. *E-mail* is the direct object. It tells what Aaron sent.
We saw him and her. *Him* and *her* are direct objects. They tell who we saw.

Circle the direct objects.

1. My friend called her and me.
2. I lost my glasses.
3. Will you visit them?
4. Jessica gave the book to him.
5. The hamster chewed the paper.
6. I sold my old car and bought a new one.
7. I lost it yesterday at the mall.
8. Doug bought some items for his new puppy.

9. The baby dropped it.
10. I like you!
11. We heard the loud siren.
12. Sue and Tina need a nap.

ACTIVITY 58 Use Objective Pronouns in Context

Name:_____

Date:_____

Direct objects are nouns or pronouns that come after an active verb to complete its meaning.

Write objective pronouns to complete the sentences. Write "O" if the objective pronoun is the object of a preposition. Write "D" if it is a direct object.

1. _____ Throw the ball to _____.
2. _____ Please give _____ to me.
3. _____ All work and no play makes _____ dull.
4. _____ Can you ride _____ to the mall?
5. _____ Will you tell _____ what happened?
6. _____ The large truck carried _____ to the factory.
7. _____ I spoke to _____ about the need for more caution.
8. _____ If you find the keys, give _____ to Dad.
9. _____ Are you looking for _____?
10. _____ I saw _____ at the library.

ACTIVITY 59 Identify Indirect Objects Name:_____

Date:_____

Indirect objects are the nouns or pronouns that come between a verb and the direct object. Indirect objects tell *to whom, to what, for whom,* or *for what* something is done. Use objective pronouns as indirect objects. A sentence may have more than one indirect object.

Examples: He told <u>me</u> a funny <u>joke</u>. *Joke* is the <u>direct</u> object.
Me is the <u>indirect</u> object. It tells to whom something was done.
She asked her <u>teacher</u> a <u>question</u>. *Question* is the <u>direct</u> object.
Teacher is the <u>indirect</u> object. It tells to whom something was done.

Circle the direct objects. Underline the indirect objects.

1. Our teacher gave her an A+ on her report.
2. They served me a wonderful meal.
3. He told me his secret.
4. Aunt Sara gave him a gift.
5. The class showed the teacher their art project.
6. That factory pays workers a good salary.
7. Uncle Joe sent his nephew a plane ticket.
8. The judge told his friend a story.
9. The principal gave the troublesome students a stern look.

ACTIVITY 60 Use Direct and Indirect   Name:_____
Objects in Context/Write a Journal Entry   Date:_____

Write a journal entry about something you did last weekend. Your entry should be at least five sentences. Continue on another sheet of paper if you need more room to write. Underline all the nouns and pronouns. Write "S" for subject, "DO" for direct object, "IO" for indirect object, or "OP" for object of a preposition to show how the nouns and pronouns are used.

    S   DO   OP   S   IO   DO
Example: <u>We</u> sailed our <u>boat</u> to my uncle's <u>island</u>. <u>He</u> promised <u>us</u> a <u>surprise</u>.

_____

_____

_____

_____

_____

_____

ACTIVITY 61   Identify Adverbs

Name: _____

Date: _____

- An **adverb** is a word that describes, limits, or makes the meaning of verbs or adjectives clearer. *Examples:* tomorrow   far   shortly   quickly   abruptly
- Adverbs answer the questions *why, where, when, how, how much,* or *how often.*
- Adverbs never describe nouns.

> *Examples:*   Yesterday, Troy ate slowly. (when; how)
>
> He usually eats quickly. (how often; how)

Underline the adverbs.

1. My sister and I often shop at the mall.

2. We rarely go to the mall on Saturday because it is too crowded.

3. Sometimes, we take my brother along.

4. We usually find interesting things on sale.

5. If we go early on a Monday, there are seldom many people at the mall.

6. Tomorrow, we will finish our chores quickly so we can go again.

7. When we walk through the mall, we will look carefully for a present for Mom.

8. Would you like to come along the next time we go to the mall?

ACTIVITY 62   Identify Adverbs

Name: _____

Date: _____

Hint: To locate adverbs, find the verb(s) in the sentence. Then look for a word or words that modifies or describes the verb.

Underline each verb. Draw an arrow to the adverbs.

> *Examples:* We will leave shortly.   Can you go tomorrow?

1. Thousands of bats flew quickly and silently from the cave.

2. Bats are nocturnal; they usually sleep during the day.

3. Some bats hibernate. They sleep deeply all winter.

4. Using sonar, bats can easily avoid flying into objects, even in the dark.

5. They often sleep in caves and usually feed at night.

6. A bat's wings are actually long fingers covered with skin.

7. Bats can't walk well.

8. People often welcome bats because they eat many harmful insects.

ACTIVITY 63 Review Adverbs and Prepositions

Name:_____

Date:_____

Some words can be used as either prepositions or adverbs.

Review what you learned about prepositional phrases and adverbs. If the underlined word is used as an adverb, write "A." If it is used as a preposition, write "P."

1. _____ Zeke took his coat <u>off</u> when he arrived.

2. _____ Can you come <u>over</u> tomorrow?

3. _____ Are you <u>through</u> with your homework?

4. _____ Can hamsters climb <u>up</u> trees?

5. _____ Please put the thread <u>through</u> the eye of the needle.

6. _____ Will you need a jacket <u>over</u> your sweater?

7. _____ Jessie was <u>behind</u> Eduardo in line.

8. _____ "You're <u>out</u>!" shouted the umpire.

9. _____ Oh no! I dropped my ring <u>down</u> the drain!

10. _____ Please take the hamster <u>out</u> for a walk.

ACTIVITY 64 Change Adjectives to Adverbs/Write Sentences

Name:_____

Date:_____

Adding a suffix to the end of a word changes the meaning of a word. Adding the suffix *-ly* to an adjective can change the adjective to an adverb. Many, but not all, adverbs end in *-ly*.

Examples: happy – happily   rare – rarely   sharp – sharply

Use the adverb form of each word in a sentence. Check a dictionary if you are not sure of the meaning or spelling of a word.

1. grateful _____

_____

2. fierce _____

_____

3. nervous _____

_____

4. polite _____

_____

ACTIVITY 65 **Identify and Write**
Comparative Adjectives

Name: _____

Date: _____

Most adjectives have three forms: **positive, comparative,** and **superlative.**
    Example: large   larger   largest
Use **comparative adjectives** to compare two people or things.
    Example: My rose is <u>red</u>.   Don's rose is <u>redder</u>.

- Add -*er* at the end of most one-syllable adjectives to form the comparative.
- For words ending in *e*, drop the *e* and add -*er*.
- For two-syllable words ending in *y*, change the *y* to *i* and add -*er*.
- For short words with the consonant/vowel/consonant (CVC) pattern, double the final consonant before adding -*er*.

Write a comparative adjective ending in -*er* to complete each sentence. Check a dictionary if you are unsure of the spelling of a word.

1. Is your computer _____ than mine?
2. Which mountain is _____, Mt. Everest or Mt. McKinley?
3. My brother is _____ than you are.
4. It often gets _____ than 100 degrees in Phoenix.
5. Who do you think will finish _____, Joan or Joel?
6. The chicken sandwich looked _____ than the hotdog.

ACTIVITY 66 **Identify and Write**
Superlative Adjectives

Name: _____

Date: _____

Use **superlative adjectives** to compare three or more people or things. To form the superlative of most adjectives, add -*est* to the end of the word. Follow the same spelling guidelines used for spelling comparative adjectives.

    Example: Which waterfall in Africa is the <u>highest</u>?

Write a superlative adjective ending in -*est* to complete each sentence.

1. What is the _____ crater on the moon?
2. What is the _____ river in China?
3. What was the _____ temperature recorded at the North Pole?
4. Of all insects, which flies the _____?
5. Heather was the _____ artist in the class.
6. November is the _____ month of the year.

Write a sentence about an animal using a superlative adjective.

_____

_____

ACTIVITY 67 Write Comparative and Superlative Adjectives

Name:_____

Date:_____

- For most two-syllable adjectives that do not end in *y*, use the words *more* and *most* for the comparative and superlative forms of adjectives.
- Form the comparative and superlative forms of adjectives with three or more syllables by combining the adjective with the word *more* or *most*.

Examples:	**Positive:**	interesting	giddy	reliable
	Comparative:	more interesting	giddier	more reliable
	Superlative:	most interesting	giddiest	most reliable

- Some adjectives have only one form.

  Examples: very   three   seventeen   first

Write the comparative and superlative forms of these adjectives. If there is only one form of the adjective, write "none" on the lines for the comparative and superlative forms. Use a dictionary if you are not sure of the spelling of a word.

Positive	Comparative	Superlative
1. jolly	_____	_____
2. fresh	_____	_____
3. gorgeous	_____	_____
4. childish	_____	_____
5. wise	_____	_____
6. last	_____	_____
7. dry	_____	_____

ACTIVITY 68 Use Irregular Adjectives in Context/Sentence Writing

Name:_____

Date:_____

A few adjectives change completely to form the comparative and superlative.

   Examples: some   more   most

Write sentences on another sheet of paper using the forms of the adjectives listed. Use a dictionary to check your answers.

1. Comparative form of *far*

2. Superlative form of *bad*

3. Superlative form of *many*

4. Comparative form of *some*

5. Superlative form of *well* (meaning *healthy*)

6. Comparative form of *little*

7. Comparative and superlative forms of *good*

ACTIVITY 69 Use Comparative and Superlative Adjectives in Context

Name: _____

Date: _____

Write the comparative or superlative form of an adjective from the list to complete each sentence.

close   good   far   hot   little   lovely   old   bad

1. I felt a _____ bit sick, Maria felt _____ sick than I did, and June felt the _____ sick of all.

2. Devan likes _____ peppers _____ than mild ones, but he likes the _____ kind _____ of all.

3. Ted is _____ to the window than Jed, and Ned is the _____ of the three.

4. Ed is the _____ student in our class.

5. Polly is 11 and Molly is 12. Molly is _____ than Polly.

6. Are you _____ than Molly?

7. Tuesday's weather was _____ than any other day this week.

8. It's _____ to drive to Iowa than to Kentucky or Tennessee.

9. Kelly had a _____ hair day today, but yesterday it was _____.

10. Yvette thinks Venus is the _____ of all the planets.

- -

ACTIVITY 70 Review Positive, Comparative, and Superlative Adjectives

Name: _____

Date: _____

Underline all of the adjectives. Write "P" for positive, "C" for comparative, or "S" for superlative above the adjectives.

1. Her fuzzy pink slippers were more shabby and worn than mine.

2. The brilliant red sunset was less spectacular than the morning's pink and purple sunrise.

3. The person with the best photograph will receive the largest prize.

4. The mail carrier delivered a red envelope to the new family in Apartment C.

5. Stan worked hard to complete the difficult project in a timely manner.

6. The Tin Man was Dorothy's best friend.

7. The Cowardly Lion asked the Wizard of Oz for more courage.

8. Although he was the most frightened, the Scarecrow was usually the smartest.

9. Dorothy was happy with her new friends, but she was happier when she returned home.

10. Oz is farther from Kansas than the moon.

ACTIVITY 71 Write Comparative and Superlative Adverbs

Name:_____

Date:_____

- Like adjectives, some adverbs have three forms.

  Examples: **Positive**   **Comparative**   **Superlative**

  often   more often   most often

  soon   sooner   soonest

- Some adverbs, such as *tomorrow*, *yesterday*, *then*, *now*, and *always* have only one form.

Review the guidelines for adding *-er* and *-est* or using *more* or *most* with comparative and superlative adjectives. Fill in the adverb chart. If there is only one form of the adverb, write "none" on the lines for the comparative and superlative forms. Use a dictionary if you need help.

Positive	Comparative	Superlative
1. brilliantly	_____	_____
2. busily	_____	_____
3. very	_____	_____
4. calmly	_____	_____
5. hastily	_____	_____
6. yesterday	_____	_____
7. silently	_____	_____
8. softly	_____	_____

ACTIVITY 72 Use Adverbs in Context

Name:_____

Date:_____

Write adverbs to complete the sentences. Underline the verbs or adjectives the adverbs modify.

1. Monica got ready _____ than her sister.

2. Martin's stomach growls _____ after he eats pizza.

3. What time will you _____ be ready to go?

4. _____, we will arrive at the airport.

5. The baby cried _____ until it fell asleep.

6. _____, I check my e-mail after school.

7. Rhonda said she was so hungry, she could _____ eat a horse.

8. Can't you move _____ than that?

9. We waited _____ for the boat to dock.

10. After we arrived in Paris, we looked _____ for a motel.

11. Ross snores _____ than a foghorn.

12. Did you sleep _____ last night?

ACTIVITY 73 Review Adjectives and

Name:_____

Prepositional Phrases/Interpret Proverbs

Date:_____

Proverbs are sayings that offer good advice or words of wisdom.

Underline all of the adjectives in these proverbs and circle the prepositional phrases. Not all sentences contain adjectives and prepositional phrases.

1. Good things come to those who wait.

2. Don't jump out of the frying pan into the fire.

3. Half of a loaf is better than none.

4. Don't cross your bridges before you come to them.

5. All work and no play makes Jack a dull boy.

6. You can't teach an old dog new tricks.

7. Inside every cloud is a silver lining.

8. People who live in glass houses should not throw stones.

9. Money is the root of all evil.

10. Great oaks from little acorns grow.

Select two of the proverbs. Rewrite the proverbs in your own words on another sheet of paper.

- -

ACTIVITY 74 Write Descriptive Sentences

Name:_____

Date:_____

Before you write about a topic, it can be helpful to make a list of related words and phrases.

If you were writing about alligators, you could begin by listing adjectives to describe their size, shape, color, and smell; nouns that relate to where they live or what they eat; and verbs to describe how they move. A dictionary and a thesaurus are useful to find synonyms and ideas.

1. Select an animal that interests you. _____

2. Write five or more adjectives that describe that animal. _____

_____   _____   _____   _____

3. Write five or more verbs that describe how that animal moves. _____

_____   _____   _____   _____

4. Write five or more nouns related to where that animal lives or what it eats.

_____   _____   _____   _____

_____

5. Use your ideas to write two sentences on another sheet of paper about the animal you chose.

ACTIVITY 75 **Write Positive,**
Comparative, and Superlative Adjectives

Name:_____

Date:_____

Make a copy of a long magazine article or short chapter from a book, or use one provided by your teacher. As you read the article, circle all of the adjectives. Underline the adverbs.

Write the adjectives from the article on the chart in the correct columns. (If an adjective is used more than once, include it only once.) For each word, fill in the other columns in the chart. If there are no comparative and superlative forms, write "none."

Positive	Comparative	Superlative

Continue on another sheet of paper if you need more room. Use the same article to complete the next activity.

- -

ACTIVITY 76 **Write Positive,**
Comparative, and Superlative Adverbs

Name:_____

Date:_____

Write the adverbs from the article used in the previous activity on the chart in the correct columns. (If an adverb is used more than once, include it only once.) For each word, fill in the other columns in the chart. If there are no comparative and superlative forms, write "none."

Positive	Comparative	Superlative

Continue on another sheet of paper if you need more room.

ACTIVITY 77 Use Conjunctions in Context/Write Causes and Effects

Name:_____

Date:_____

Conjunctions connect two or more words or groups of words.
> *And, but, or, nor, so,* and *because* are conjunctions.
>> *Examples:* We will go to the pet store, <u>so</u> we can choose a new pet.
>> I would like a dog, cat, <u>or</u> canary, <u>but</u> not a snake.
>> <u>Neither</u> a snake <u>nor</u> a hamster would be my first choice for a pet.

Finish the sentences by writing a conjunction.

1. Vicky decided to get a pet _____ she was lonely.
2. Vicky was lonely, _____ she decided to get a pet.
3. Vicky decided to get a pet, _____ she did not want a canary.

Because or *so* are used in sentences that show cause and effect.
> *Examples:* We had 18 inches of snow,   /   <u>so</u> we spent all day shoveling.
> (cause)   (effect)

Write an effect for each cause.

4. Tori overslept, so _____.
5. _____ because she overslept.

Write a cause for each effect.

6. Jason felt sick because _____.
7. Jason felt sick, so _____.

ACTIVITY 78 Use Conjunctions in Context/Write Sentences

Name:_____

Date:_____

Conjunctions connect two or more words or groups of words.
> *Examples:* Toby will return a book to the library, go jogging, <u>and</u> visit his dad.
> Toby will return the book to the library, go jogging, <u>or</u> visit his dad.

Write a sentence using each conjunction to join two or more groups of words.

1. and _____
   _____

2. or _____
   _____

3. nor _____
   _____

4. but _____
   _____

5. because _____
   _____

6. so _____
   _____

ACTIVITY 79 Use Conjunctions To Write Compound Sentences

Name:_____

Date:_____

Conjunctions can join two or more short sentences.

- Join two short sentences with *and* when the sentences are similar.
  Example: Josh painted a birdhouse, <u>and</u> he built a chicken coop.
- Join two short sentences with *but* when the second sentence contradicts the first.
  Example: Josh painted a birdhouse, <u>but</u> he did not build a chicken coop.
- Join two short sentences with *or* when they name a choice.
  Example: Josh will paint a birdhouse, <u>or</u> he will build a chicken coop.
- Join two short sentences with *because* or *so* when the second one names a reason for the first one.
  Example: Josh painted the birdhouse <u>because</u> he enjoys watching birds.

Add another short sentence after each conjunction to finish each sentence.

1. Lana will go for a hike in the woods, or _____

   _____

2. Lana will go for a hike in the woods because _____

   _____

3. Lana will go for a hike in the woods, and _____

   _____

- -

ACTIVITY 80 Use Conjunctions in Context/Write a Journal Entry

Name:_____

Date:_____

Write a journal entry about a real or imaginary trip to an imaginary place. Use conjunctions to join words, phrases, or short sentences. Underline the conjunctions.

_____

_____

_____

_____

_____

_____

_____

_____

_____

_____

Continue writing on another sheet of paper if you need more room.

ACTIVITY 81 Review Prepositional
Phrases and Pronouns/Test-Taking

Name:_____

Date:_____

Circle "T" for true or "F" for false.

1. T   F   A direct object is a noun or pronoun that comes after an active verb to complete its meaning. It answers the question *who* or *what.*
2. T   F   A phrase is the same as a sentence.
3. T   F   A phrase that begins with a preposition is a prepositional phrase only if it includes a noun or pronoun.
4. T   F   All prepositional phrases must begin with a preposition and include at least one verb.
5. T   F   An indirect object is a noun or pronoun that comes between a verb and the direct object and tells *to whom, to what, for whom,* or *for what* something is done.
6. T   F   Any pronoun, including *we, he, you,* and *they,* can be used as the direct object in a sentence.
7. T   F   *I* is a singular pronoun, but it uses a plural verb.
8. T   F   *I, me, you, him, her,* and *it* are singular pronouns.
9. T   F   If a singular noun is masculine or feminine, use a masculine or feminine pronoun. Otherwise, use *it.*
10. T   F   The object of a preposition is the noun or pronoun that follows a preposition and is part of the prepositional phrase.
11. T   F   The pronoun *you* is always plural.
12. T   F   Two or more pronouns can be the objects of one preposition.

ACTIVITY 82 Review Parts of Speech/
Test-Taking

Name:_____

Date:_____

Write the word from the list that names all words in each set. Words may be used more than once.

adjectives   adverbs   conjunctions   common nouns

prepositions   pronouns   proper nouns   verbs

1. _____ slow, firm, first, clear
2. _____ rescue, be, went, traveled
3. _____ they, us, we, it
4. _____ is, can, has, were
5. _____ castle, athlete, happiness
6. _____ February, Mississippi, Uncle Sean
7. _____ inside, around, through, behind
8. _____ and, but, or, nor, so, because
9. _____ soon, yesterday, seldom, gracefully
10. _____ for, without, into, throughout
11. _____ tomorrow, near, out, brightly
12. _____ I, them, she, you
13. _____ hamster, opera, independence

adjectives

verbs

adverbs

ACTIVITY 83 Correct Run-On Sentences

Name:_____

Date:_____

A **run-on sentence** occurs when two or more sentences are joined together without punctuation or conjunctions.

Examples: **Run-on sentence:**   I finished my report did you?
Correct punctuation: I finished my report. Did you?
Run-on sentence: I washed the dishes my brother dried them.
Sentence with conjunction: I washed the dishes, and my brother dried them.

Rewrite the run-on sentences on on your own paper using conjunctions and/or punctuation.

1. Do you know where Todd went I can't find him anywhere.

2. How can you eat that stinky cheese I can't!

3. Look out that water is very deep.

4. My hamster ran out the door did you see which way he went will he get lost?

5. The sky got darker the snow began to fall the sidewalks were soon covered the roads became slippery.

ACTIVITY 84 Review Sentence Writing

Name:_____

Date:_____

- A sentence can include two or more nouns as subjects.
  Example: Peter, Paul, and Mary sang folk songs.
- A sentence can include two or more verbs.
  Example: Justin Case won the race and received the trophy.

Write sentences that include the parts of speech listed.

1. Two or more nouns and one verb _____

_____

2. Two or more nouns and two or more verbs _____

_____

3. Three or more adjectives, one noun, and two verbs _____

_____

4. A noun, a verb, and an adverb _____

_____

ACTIVITY 85 Use Interrogative/ Subjective Pronouns

Name:_____

Date:_____

An **interrogative pronoun** introduces a question. *Who*, *what*, and *which* are interrogative pronouns that can be used as subjects of a sentence.

- Use *who* when speaking of people.
- Use *what* when speaking of things.
- Use *which* when speaking of groups or things.

<u>Who</u> will try the hot mustard?
<u>What</u> is in the hot mustard?
<u>Which</u> came first, the chicken or the egg?

Write "who," "what," or "which" to complete the sentences.

1. _____ did she do then?
2. _____ dropped the ball?
3. _____ flavor of ice cream do you prefer?
4. _____ plan do you like best?
5. _____ team won?
6. _____ will happen at midnight?
7. _____ will you do now?
8. Can you tell _____ of the horses will win the race?
9. Did you see _____ came in first?

ACTIVITY 86 Use Various Forms of Interrogative Pronouns

Name:_____

Date:_____

- Use *whom* instead of *who* as the object of a preposition.
    Example: To <u>whom</u> did you send the letter?
- *What* and *which* can be used as subjects, direct objects, or objects of a preposition.
    Example: To <u>what</u> do I owe this honor?
- The possessive form of *whom* is *whose*.

Circle the correct word in each sentence.

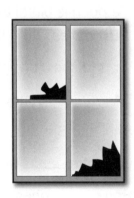

1. (Who / Whom) broke the window?
2. We all know (who / whom) will be ready on time.
3. To (who / whom) should I give the package?
4. (Who / Whose) drawing is this?
5. For (who / whom) is the present?
6. (What / Whose) were you thinking?
7. Ask not for (who / whom) the bell tolls.
8. Do you know (whose / who) started the rumor?
9. You dropped (what / who) in the lake?
10. (Who / What) will Terra choose for dinner?

ACTIVITY 87   Review Sentence Writing   Name:_____

Date:_____

1. Write an interrogative sentence. Include at least one prepositional phrase.

   _____

   _____

2. Write a declarative sentence that uses two or more adverbs.

   _____

   _____

3. Write an imperative sentence that uses two or more nouns as objects of a preposition.

   _____

   _____

4. Write an interrogative sentence that includes a conjunction and an interrogative pronoun.

   _____

   _____

5. Write a sentence that includes a direct and indirect object and one or more adjectives.

   _____

   _____

ACTIVITY 88   Use Apostrophes to   Name:_____
Show Ownership

Date:_____

Use an **apostrophe** to show ownership with nouns.

- If a noun is singular, add *'s* to show ownership, even if the noun ends in *s*.

   Examples: the boss's office   Doug and Dan's brother   the skunk's stripe

- If a noun is plural and ends in *s*, add only an apostrophe.

   Examples: the girls' friend   the Browns' vacation   the dogs' home

Add *'* or *'s* to show ownership.

1. Barry_____ bunny

2. Shel and Sid_____ snails

3. Charlotte_____ web

4. Ron_____ robes

5. the sentence_____ subject

6. the class_____ assignment

7. Ross_____ backyard

8. the trees_____ leaves

9. the bees_____ knees

10. the cat_____ pajamas

11. the world_____ population

12. the monkey_____ eyebrow

ACTIVITY 89 Use Apostrophes to Show Ownership

Name:_____

Date:_____

Use an **apostrophe** to show ownership with nouns.

- If a noun is plural and does not end in *s*, add *'s*.
    Examples: the people's choice   the children's teacher
- Do not use an apostrophe with pronouns to show ownership.
    Examples: its tail and feathers   their basketball

Write the plural for each noun. Add *'* or *'s* to show ownership. Use a dictionary if you need help spelling the plural.

1. wife _____ photographs
2. man _____ golf clubs
3. mouse _____ ears
4. wolf _____ howls
5. person _____ house
6. foot _____ toenails

7. bunny _____ ears
8. attorney _____ books
9. box _____ lids
10. goose _____ feathers
11. volcano _____ lava
12. hero _____ feats

ACTIVITY 90 Form Singular and Plural Possessive Nouns

Name:_____

Date:_____

- One person or thing can possess more than one thing.
    Examples: Tim's bats and balls   the bird's feathers
- More than one person can possess one item.
    Examples: the children's mother   the rabbits' den
- When two or more nouns are connected with *and*, only the last noun in the series changes to possessive form.
    Examples: the boys and girls' playground   Pete, Paul, and Patti's parents

Write two examples for each type.

Singular noun, singular item possessed

_____

_____

Singular noun, plural items possessed

_____

_____

Plural noun, singular item possessed

_____

_____

Plural noun, plural items possessed

_____

_____

Two or more nouns connected with *and*, singular item possessed

_____

_____

Two or more nouns connected with *and*, plural items possessed

_____

_____

ACTIVITY 91 Identify/Use Possessive
Pronouns

Name:_____

Date:_____

- **Pronouns** are words that can take the place of nouns.
  Examples: Kim and Amy's books – their books   the elephant's trunk – its trunk
- **Possessive pronouns** show ownership.
  Singular: my, mine, your, yours, her, hers, his, its
  Plural: our, ours, your, yours, their, theirs
- Use a **singular** pronoun if the person, place, or thing that owns something is <u>singular</u>.
  Example: Bo Peep lost <u>her</u> sheep.   The lost sheep were <u>hers</u>.
- Use a plural pronoun if something belongs to people, places, or things.
  Example: Miss Muffet and the spider ate <u>their</u> curds and whey.
             The curds and whey were <u>theirs</u>.

Write possessive pronouns to complete the sentences.

1. The chickens that belong to Brita are _____ chickens. The chickens are
   _____.
2. The flowers I planted are _____ flowers. The flowers are _____.
3. The house Tim built is _____ house. The house is _____.
4. The computer that belongs to you and me is _____ computer. The computer is
   _____.
5. The software that belongs to Ted and Tina is _____ software. The software is
   _____.

ACTIVITY 92 Use Possessive Pronouns
in Context/Write Sentences

Name:_____

Date:_____

Write short sentences using the possessive pronouns listed.

her   _____

hers   _____

his   _____

its   _____

mine   _____

my   _____

our   _____

ours   _____

their _____

theirs _____

yours _____

your   _____

ACTIVITY 93   Review Subjective, Possessive, and Objective Pronouns

Name:_____

Date:_____

Write the pronouns from the list that fit into each group. Some pronouns fit into more than one group.

he	her	hers	him	his	I	it	its	me	mine	my	our
ours	she	their	theirs	them	they	us	we	you	your	yours	

Singular subjective pronouns _____

Plural subjective pronouns _____

Singular objective pronouns _____

Plural objective pronouns _____

Singular possessive pronouns _____

Plural possessive pronouns _____

Male pronouns _____

Female pronouns _____

- -

ACTIVITY 94   Use Pronouns in Context

Name:_____

Date:_____

Pronouns make our writing more interesting. We use pronouns to avoid using the same noun several times in a sentence.

Rewrite the sentences using pronouns to simplify.

Example: Jane saw Jane's brother throw Jane's brother's ball to Jane's best friend.
Jane saw her brother throw his ball to her best friend.

1. Sara Simpson gave Sara Simpson's sister singing lessons at Sara Simpson's sister's house. _____

_____

2. The two toads took the two toads' toadstools to the two toads' teacher.

_____

_____

3. Marvin married Mabel, and Marvin and Mabel moved to Miami where Marvin and Mabel lived in a motel for a month.

_____

_____

4. In September, Sam sold the stamps that belonged to Sam to Sam's sister Sue.

_____

_____

ACTIVITY 95   Use Contractions in Context

Name:_____

Date:_____

Contractions are two words joined together. An **apostrophe** shows that letters are missing. Many contractions include the word *not*.

are not = aren't	cannot = can't	could not = couldn't
did not = didn't	do not = don't	does not = doesn't
has not = hasn't	have not = haven't	is not = isn't
should not = shouldn't	was not = wasn't	will not = won't
would not = wouldn't		

Write contractions to finish these proverbs.

1.   A leopard _____ change its spots.
2.   _____ look a gift horse in the mouth.
3.   Money _____ grow on trees.
4.   People who live in glass houses _____ throw stones.
5.   You _____ teach an old dog new tricks.
6.   _____ bite off more than you can chew.

Give several reasons why you think we use contractions when speaking and writing.

_____

_____

ACTIVITY 96   Use Contractions in Context/Write Interrogative Sentences

Name:_____

Date:_____

Write interrogative sentences using contractions for the words listed.

1.   are not _____

_____

2.   could not _____

_____

3.   has not _____

_____

4.   have not _____

_____

5.   should not _____

_____

6.   was not _____

_____

7.   will not _____

_____

ACTIVITY 97 Use Contractions in Context

Name:_____

Date:_____

Contractions are two words joined together. An **apostrophe** shows that letters are missing. Many contractions include pronouns:

I am = I'm	he is = he's	she is = she's	it is = it's
I will = I'll	he will = he'll	she will = she'll	it has = it's
I would = I'd	he would = he'd	she would = she'd	
I have = I've	he has = he's	she has = she's	
we are = we're	they are = they're	you are = you're	
we will = we'll	they will = they'll	you will = you'll	
we would = we'd	they would = they'd	you would = you'd	
we have = we've	they have = they've	you have = you've	

Write contractions to finish the sentences.

1. _____ time to wake up.
2. _____ be there tomorrow.
3. _____ help weed the garden.
4. _____ eaten too much pizza.
5. _____ need to be there early.
6. _____ too much work to do.
7. _____ going water skiing today.
8. _____ welcome to come.

ACTIVITY 98 Write Contractions/ Use Contractions in Context

Name:_____

Date:_____

Write the contractions for the words. Use a dictionary if you are unsure of the spelling.

1. _____ how is
2. _____ how will
3. _____ that is
4. _____ that has
5. _____ there is
6. _____ what will
7. _____ where is
8. _____ where has
9. _____ why did
10. _____ who is
11. _____ who would
12. _____ how did
13. _____ let us
14. _____ that will
15. _____ there are
16. _____ what is
17. _____ what has
18. _____ where did
19. _____ when is
20. _____ who has
21. _____ who will
22. _____ why is

On your own paper, write three sentences using any of the contractions from the list above.

ACTIVITY 99 Differentiate Between Pronouns and Contractions

Name:_____

Date:_____

Homophones are words that sound the same, but are spelled differently.

Examples: sale and sail   aye and eye   you and ewe

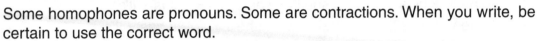

Some homophones are pronouns. Some are contractions. When you write, be certain to use the correct word.

Write the word from the list that matches the definition. Not all the words will be used. Use a dictionary if you are not sure of the meaning of a word.

aye	ewe	eye	him	hours	hymn	I	its	it's	ours
theirs	there	there's	they're	we	wee	yew	you	your	you're

1. _____ a male singular pronoun
2. _____ a type of bush
3. _____ very small
4. _____ subjective plural pronoun
5. _____ belongs to you
6. _____ contraction for *there is*
7. _____ contraction for *they are*
8. _____ contraction for *you are*

9. _____ in that place
10. _____ belongs to it
11. _____ a song of praise
12. _____ opposite of me
13. _____ female sheep
14. _____ belongs to them
15. _____ yes
16. _____ contraction for *it is*

ACTIVITY 100 Differentiate Between Possessive Nouns and Contractions

Name:_____

Date:_____

Apostrophes are used in contractions and to show possession.

Write "C" for contraction or "P" for possessive to indicate how the underlined words are used. If the word is a contraction, write out the words for the contractions after the sentence.

1. _____ A <u>man's</u> reach should exceed his grasp.   _____

2. _____ When the <u>cat's</u> away, the mice will play.   _____

3. _____ <u>It's</u> the thought that counts.   _____

4. _____ The <u>check's</u> in the mail.   _____

5. _____ <u>You're</u> only young once.   _____

6. _____ <u>You're</u> never too old to learn.   _____

7. _____ <u>What's</u> good for the goose is good for the gander.   _____

8. _____ <u>Nobody's</u> perfect.   _____

9. _____ <u>There's</u> no place like home.   _____

10. _____ <u>Two's</u> company, <u>three's</u> a crowd.   _____ _____

11. _____ Where <u>there's</u> a will, <u>there's</u> a way.   _____ _____

12. _____ His <u>bark's</u> worse than his bite.   _____

ACTIVITY 101 Use Commas in Direct Address

Name: _____

Date: _____

A noun in **direct address** names the person to whom you are speaking in a sentence. Use commas to separate nouns in direct address from the rest of the sentence. Both common and proper nouns can be used in direct address.

Examples: Your hamster, <u>Herman</u>, is a nuisance.
<u>Herman</u>, your hamster is a nuisance.
Your hamster is a nuisance, <u>Herman</u>.

Add commas to separate the words used in direct address.

1. Alice where are you going?
2. Well dear what do you have to say for yourself?
3. Listen up class. Tomorrow, we will have a test.
4. Derek would you like to meet me at the library?
5. I can help you Raphael, but I'm afraid I can't help you too Monica.
6. Alice and Fay come to the principal's office at once.
7. Would you like to ride with Dad to the mall Kay?
8. Did you Paul plant those purple petunias?
9. Alicia you ate eight cookies. That's enough.
10. Attention everyone. This is not a drill class.

ACTIVITY 102 Use Commas With Appositives

Name: _____

Date: _____

Appositives are words that provide more information about a previous noun or pronoun. Use commas to separate appositives from the rest of the sentence.

Examples: Herman, <u>my youngest brother</u>, has a hamster named Helen.
My math book, <u>the one I used last year</u>, is under the sofa.

Underline the words used as appositives. Add commas as needed.

1. What is the capital of Texas Austin or Houston?
2. Tick Bite a town in North Carolina and Hot Coffee a town in Mississippi are two places with unusual names.
3. The green tree frog the official state amphibian of Georgia and Louisiana is a type of frog found in temperate and tropical areas throughout the world
4. Connecticut officially nicknamed the Constitution State is also known as the Nutmeg State.
5. No one seems to know why Indiana known as the Hoosier State has that nickname.
6. Milk the official state beverage of many states is better for you than soda.
7. Only one state Florida has orange juice as its official state beverage.
8. Cranberry juice the official state beverage of Massachusetts and tomato juice the state beverage of Ohio are unusual, but not as strange as the state soft drink of Nebraska.

ACTIVITY 103 Differentiate Between
Direct Address And Appositives

Name:_____

Date:_____

Underline words used in direct address or as appositives and add commas. Write "DA" if the sentence contains words used in direct address or "A" if the sentence contains an appositive.

1. _____ Harry Potter the boy who lived made friends with many students at Hogwarts.
2. _____ It's time to go to the fair Charlotte.
3. _____ You cannot lasso a tornado Pecos Bill.
4. _____ Spiderman originally a character in comic books became a movie hero.
5. Write two sentences that use a noun in direct address. Add commas as needed.

_____

_____

_____

_____

6. Write two sentences that use appositives. Add commas as needed.

_____

_____

_____

_____

ACTIVITY 104 Review Contractions/
Test-Taking

Name:_____

Date:_____

Write contractions for the words.

1. are not _____
2. she will _____
3. has not _____
4. I will _____
5. they will _____
6. would not _____
7. he would _____
8. you have _____
9. how is _____
10. who will _____

Write words for the contractions.

11. wasn't _____
12. there's _____
13. don't _____
14. I'd _____
15. they've _____
16. that's _____
17. you'd _____
18. aren't _____
19. let's _____
20. won't _____

ACTIVITY 105 **Review Definitions/**   Name: _____
Test-Taking   Date: _____

Write words from the list to match the definitions. Words may be used more than once.

active verbs	adverbs	apostrophes	appositives	conjunctions
contractions	prepositions	proper nouns	suffixes	

1. _____ answer the questions *why, where, when, how, how much,* or *how often*
2. _____ can change an adjective to an adverb
3. _____ change the meaning of a word
4. _____ connect words or groups of words
5. _____ describe the size, shape, color, or number of someone or something
6. _____ describe, limit, or make the meanings of verbs or adjectives clearer
7. _____ include positive, comparative, and superlative forms
8. _____ name specific people, places, or things
9. _____ provide more information about a previous noun or pronoun
10. _____ tell what someone or something did, does, or will do
11. _____ two words joined together, but with letters missing
12. _____ used to show possession
13. _____ used to show that letters are missing in a contraction
14. _____ words that come before a noun or pronoun and introduce a phrase

- -

ACTIVITY 106 **Review Parts of Speech/** Name: _____
Test-Taking   Date: _____

Circle "T" for true or "F" for false.

1. T F Apostrophes are used to set off appositives from the rest of the sentence.
2. T F Verbs can be present, past, or future tense.
3. T F Irregular verbs form the past tense by adding *-ed.*
4. T F Inactive verbs are often used as linking verbs.
5. T F Inactive verbs express a state of being.
6. T F The most common inactive verbs are forms of the word *go.*
7. T F Add *s* to most verbs to change them from singular to plural.
8. T F *Who, what, which,* and *whom* are interrogative pronouns.
9. T F Use *who* as the object of a preposition.
10. T F If a noun is plural and ends in an *s,* add *'es* to form the possessive.
11. T F Add *'s* to all nouns and pronouns to form the possessive form.
12. T F A noun in direct address names the person to whom you are speaking in a sentence.
13. T F Homophones are words that sound the same, but are spelled differently.
14. T F Any two words can be changed to a contraction if one is a noun and the other a verb.

Who?

Which?

What?

ACTIVITY 107 Determine Parts of Speech of Words

Name: _____

Date: _____

Some words have more than one meaning and can be used as either a noun or a verb. Clues in the sentence help you decide how the word is used.

Write "N" if the boldface word is a noun. Write "V" if it is a verb. Use a dictionary if you are not sure of the meaning of a word or how it is used.

1. _____ Marcus and his **associates** brainstormed for new ideas.
2. _____ I **challenge** you to complete this puzzle.
3. _____ Many male birds put on a fancy courtship **display**.
4. _____ Can you **estimate** the cost of a new roof?
5. _____ Which **experiment** did you find most interesting?
6. _____ Can you **influence** your friends to join the chess club?
7. _____ How much **influence** do your friends have on your actions?
8. _____ Phil **associates** with many other professors on a regular basis.
9. _____ Are you up for this **challenge**?
10. _____ The art teacher will **display** the paintings in the library.
11. _____ Hannah often **experiments** with new recipes.
12. _____ The contractor gave us an **estimate** of what the new roof would cost.

ACTIVITY 108 Use Words as Different Parts of Speech/Write Sentences

Name: _____

Date: _____

Write a sentence for each word. Use a dictionary if you need help.

1. auction (as a noun) _____

_____

2. auction (as a verb) _____

_____

3. answer (as a noun) _____

_____

4. answer (as a verb) _____

_____

5. boycott (as a noun) _____

_____

6. boycott (as a verb) _____

_____

7. thought (as a noun) _____

_____

8. thought (as a verb) _____

_____

ACTIVITY 109   Use Words as Different

Name:_____

Date:_____

Parts of Speech/Write Sentences

Some words can be used as nouns, verbs, and adjectives.

Examples: Brown is my favorite color. (noun)
Please brown the meat so I can make the spaghetti sauce. (verb)
My puppy has brown spots. (adjective)

Write short sentences using the words as the parts of speech listed. Use a dictionary if you need help.

1. draft (noun)_____

_____

2. draft (verb) _____

_____

3. draft (adjective) _____

_____

4. salt (noun) _____

_____

5. salt (verb) _____

_____

6. salt (adjective) _____

_____

ACTIVITY 110   Classify Words With

Name:_____

Date:_____

Multiple Meanings

On another sheet of paper, write the headings below. Write words from the list for each group. Words may be used in more than one group. Use a dictionary if you need help.

1. Words from the list that are verbs
2. Ten other words that are verbs
3. Words from the list that are nouns
4. Ten other words that are nouns
5. Words from the list that are adjectives
6. Ten other words that are adjectives

answer	arch	blend	blooms	brown	call	can
clean	clutch	coast	commercial	complex	computer	cook
dance	debate	design	dice	digest	drop	duck
exhaust	experience	focus	frost	fuel	guard	hand
issue	latch	loom	offer	orange	paint	
patient	pilot	plow	post	range	safe	
scoop	second	secure	sketch	sleep	sprout	
stall	stock	stop	terminal	trial		

ACTIVITY 111 Write Synonyms for Verbs

Name:_____

Date:_____

Synonyms are words that mean the same, or nearly the same.
Examples: Stare, gaze, watch, see, and *glance* are synonyms for *look.*

Write three or more synonyms for each verb. Use a dictionary or thesaurus
to find words if you need help.

1. take _____

2. speak _____

3. leave _____

4. understand _____

5. locate _____

6. work _____

7. give _____

8. go/went _____

9. shake _____

10. ask _____

ACTIVITY 112 Use Interesting Verbs/
Sentence Writing

Name:_____

Date:_____

Using a variety of strong action verbs helps make your writing more interesting.
Examples: Tremble, whirl, shiver, frolic, and *shriek* are interesting verbs.

Use lively, exciting verbs to change dull sentences to interesting ones.
Example: **Dull:**   Alex was excited.
              Interesting: Alex quivered with suppressed excitement.

Rewrite the sentences to make them more interesting by using action verbs.

1. Edward was sad. _____

    _____

2. Emily was scared. _____

    _____

3. Jeremy was hungry. _____

    _____

4. The puppies were lonely. _____

    _____

5. "I am fine," he said. _____

    _____

ACTIVITY 113 Write Synonyms for Adjectives

Name:_____

Date:_____

Adding a variety of interesting adjectives provides the reader with a very clear word picture.

Example: **Vague:**   The puppy sat by Grandpa's chair.

Specific: The lonely puppy with large, sad, brown eyes and droopy ears sat by Grandpa's empty chair.

Write three or more synonyms for each adjective. Use a dictionary or thesaurus to find words if you need help.

1. sad _____

2. quick _____

3. large _____

4. slow _____

5. nice _____

Rewrite the sentences on another sheet of paper using a variety of interesting adjectives.

6. The students presented good reports.

7. We had a good time watching the elephants at the circus.

ACTIVITY 114 Write Synonyms for Nouns

Name:_____

Date:_____

The words *boy, girl, toddler, teenager, youngster, tot, baby,* and *infant* are synonyms for *child.* Although each of the words is similar in meaning, using the exact words is also important. Replacing words with synonyms can provide a more specific word picture.

1. Read the sentences. Explain how changing the word *child* changes the entire meaning.

The <u>child</u> sobbed uncontrollably.

The <u>baby girl</u> sobbed uncontrollably.

The <u>toddler</u> sobbed uncontrollably.

The <u>teenage boy</u> sobbed uncontrollably.

_____

_____

_____

_____

On another sheet of paper, write three or more synonyms for each noun. Use a dictionary or thesaurus if you need help.

2. adult   3. bridge   4. party   5. courtesy

6. fun   7. chores   8. meeting

ACTIVITY 115   Write Antonyms

Name:_____

Date:_____

Antonyms are words that mean the opposite.
Examples: questions and answers
wake and sleep
forward and backward

Write words that are antonyms. Use a dictionary or a thesaurus if you are unsure of the meaning of a word.

1. _____ expensive
2. _____ aware
3. _____ wealthy
4. _____ expected
5. _____ regular
6. _____ thaw
7. _____ difficult
8. _____ freedom
9. _____ interior
10. _____ inhale

11. _____ construct
12. _____ contract
13. _____ convex
14. _____ acquire
15. _____ broken
16. _____ contradict
17. _____ defy
18. _____ exceed
19. _____ unify
20. _____ slouch

ACTIVITY 116   Write Antonyms
and Synonyms

Name:_____

Date:_____

Synonyms are words that mean the same or nearly the same.

Antonyms are words that mean the opposite.

Write a synonym and an antonym for each word. Use a dictionary if you are unsure of the meaning of a word.

	Antonyms	**Synonyms**
1. absurd	_____	_____
2. aloof	_____	_____
3. dense	_____	_____
4. dreadful	_____	_____
5. energetic	_____	_____
6. familiar	_____	_____
7. frail	_____	_____
8. gracious	_____	_____
9. grateful	_____	_____
10. jagged	_____	_____

ACTIVITY 117 Recognize Antonyms and Synonyms

Name:_____

Date:_____

Circle all words in each row that are **antonyms** for the first word. Use a dictionary if you're not sure of the meaning of a word.

1.	capable	unable	able	powerless	incapable
2.	defiant	hostile	friendly	aggressive	pleasant
3.	deliberate	purposeful	careless	hasty	careful
4.	hasty	quick	slow	leisurely	careful
5.	hesitant	certain	cautious	sure	definite
6.	thoughtful	concerned	unkind	inconsiderate	mean
7.	knowledgeable	unaware	smart	uninformed	ignorant

Circle all words in each row that are **synonyms** for the first word. Use a dictionary if you aren't sure of the meaning of a word.

8.	jubilant	sad	joyful	happy	depressed
9.	fidget	squirm	wiggle	unmoving	motionless
10.	release	capture	detain	free	liberate
11.	hostile	defiant	friendly	kindly	enemy
12.	irritate	soothe	annoy	bother	pacify
13.	meddle	interfere	pry	assist	hinder
14.	enforce	impose	require	inflict	release

ACTIVITY 118 Recognize Antonyms and Synonyms

Name:_____

Date:_____

Write "A" if the words are antonyms or "S" if the words are synonyms. Use a dictionary if you are not sure of the meaning of a word.

1. _____ absurd and ridiculous
2. _____ dense and thick
3. _____ friendly and aloof
4. _____ great and tremendous
5. _____ kind and gracious
6. _____ luxurious and elegant
7. _____ shoddy and luxurious
8. _____ strong and frail
9. _____ terrific and dreadful
10. _____ thankless and grateful
11. _____ tired and energetic
12. _____ weak and frail

13. _____ aloof and distant
14. _____ familiar and known
15. _____ gracious and unkind
16. _____ jagged and broken
17. _____ lively and energetic
18. _____ reasonable and absurd
19. _____ smooth and jagged
20. _____ terrible and dreadful
21. _____ thankful and grateful
22. _____ thin and dense
23. _____ unknown and familiar
24. _____ wonderful and tremendous

ACTIVITY 119 Define Homophones

Name:_____

Date:_____

Homophones are words that sound the same, but are spelled differently and have different meanings. Correct writing and grammar includes using the correct words.

Write the homophones from the list next to their definitions. Use a dictionary if you aren't sure of a word.

base	bass	beau	bow	boy	buoy
pries	principal	principle	prize	seas	seize
straight	strait	threw	through		

1. _____ sea marker
2. _____ young male
3. _____ snoops
4. _____ most important
5. _____ tossed
6. _____ lowest musical tones
7. _____ to grab
8. _____ finished

9. _____ tied ribbon
10. _____ narrow passage
11. _____ bottom support
12. _____ head of a school
13. _____ not crooked
14. _____ award
15. _____ bodies of water
16. _____ boyfriend

ACTIVITY 120 Write and Define Homophones

Name:_____

Date:_____

Write a short definition for each word. Then write a homophone for the word and a definition for the homophone. Use a dictionary if you need help.

	Word	Definition	Homophone	Definition
1.	arc	_____	_____	_____
2.	ascent	_____	_____	_____
3.	bail	_____	_____	_____
4.	band	_____	_____	_____
5.	berry	_____	_____	_____
6.	cell	_____	_____	_____
7.	chili	_____	_____	_____
8.	coarse	_____	_____	_____
9.	feat	_____	_____	_____
10.	might	_____	_____	_____
11.	role	_____	_____	_____
12.	wait	_____	_____	_____

ACTIVITY 121   Use Homophones in Context/Write Sentences

Name:_____

Date:_____

Write short sentences using each homophone correctly. Use a dictionary if you are not sure of a word.

1. boar _____
2. bore _____
3. hole _____
4. whole _____
5. stair _____
6. stare _____
7. steal _____
8. steel _____
9. vain _____
10. vane _____
11. waist _____
12. waste _____

ACTIVITY 122   Define Homophones

Name:_____

Date:_____

Write a short definition for each homophone. Use a dictionary if you are not sure of the meaning of a word.

1. rays _____
2. raze _____
3. raise _____
4. vary _____
5. very _____
6. lesson _____
7. lessen _____
8. grate _____
9. great _____
10. vane _____
11. vain _____
12. vein _____

ACTIVITY 123 Write Antonyms of Homophones

Name: _____

Date: _____

Write the letter of the homophone that is an **antonym** for the word in the first column. Use a dictionary if you need help.

#	word	a.	b.
1.	____ lose	a. find	b. fined
2.	____ hot	a. chili	b. chilly
3.	____ daughter	a. son	b. sun
4.	____ day	a. knight	b. night
5.	____ female	a. mail	b. male
6.	____ go	a. wait	b. weight
7.	____ low	a. hi	b. high
8.	____ whole	a. peace	b. piece
9.	____ open	a. close	b. clothes
10.	____ increase	a. lesson	b. lessen
11.	____ save	a. waist	b. waste
12.	____ strong	a. weak	b. week
13.	____ toe	a. heel	b. heal
14.	____ war	a. peace	b. piece

ACTIVITY 124 Write Synonyms of Homophones

Name: _____

Date: _____

Write the letter of the homophone that is a **synonym** for the word in the first column. Use a dictionary if you need help.

#	word	a.	b.	c.
1.	____ male pig	a. bore	b. boar	
2.	____ musicians	a. band	b. banned	
3.	____ wood	a. board	b. bored	
4.	____ an animal	a. links	b. lynx	
5.	____ rules	a. rains	b. reigns	c. reins
6.	____ moisture	a. due	b. do	c. dew
7.	____ a pronoun	a. ewe	b. you	c. yew
8.	____ a fruit	a. pair	b. pare	c. pear
9.	____ a number	a. for	b. four	c. fore
10.	____ pennies	a. cents	b. sense	c. scents
11.	____ odors	a. cents	b. sense	c. scents
12.	____ an animal	a. gnu	b. new	c. knew
13.	____ a number	a. to	b. two	c. too
14.	____ farewell	a. by	b. bye	c. buy
15.	____ not rich	a. poor	b. pour	c. pore

ACTIVITY 125 Review Homophones/ Test-Taking

Name:_____

Date:_____

Match the homophones with their definitions.

1. _____ bail   a. forbidden
2. _____ band   b. rob
3. _____ boar   c. contraction for *you are*
4. _____ ewe   d. bundle
5. _____ its   e. contraction for *they are*
6. _____ lessen   f. cold
7. _____ steal   g. belongs to them
8. _____ their   h. contraction for *it is*
9. _____ they're   i. belongs to it
10. _____ yew   j. a golf ball holder

11. _____ your   k. group of musicians
12. _____ bale   l. strong metal
13. _____ banned   m. type of bush
14. _____ chilly   n. reduce
15. _____ hour   o. remove water
16. _____ it's   p. class
17. _____ lesson   q. 60 minutes
18. _____ steel   r. male pig
19. _____ tee   s. belongs to you
20. _____ you're   t. female sheep

ACTIVITY 126 Identify and Classify Compound Words

Name:_____

Date:_____

A **compound word** combines two or more words to make a new word that expresses a single idea. *Newborn, keepsake,* and *friendship* are compound words.

Use a dictionary to complete this activity if you need help.

1. Draw lines to separate the two words that make up each compound word.
2. Circle the compound words that name animals/insects.
3. Underline the compound words that are food.
4. Make a check mark in front of the compound words that are places, such as rooms, countries, etc.
5. Write the compound word that does not fit into any of the three categories above.

_____

applesauce	backyard	bedroom	bulldog	butterfly	courthouse
cupcake	elbow room	farmyard	firefly	gooseberry	grapefruit
greenhouse	Greenland	hedgehog	Hollywood	Iceland	horseradish
inchworm	jellyfish	ladybug	lighthouse	Maryland	meatloaf
oatmeal	outhouse	pineapple	polecat	popcorn	Portland
potpie	rattlesnake	roadrunner	sapsucker	shortcake	silkworm
starfish	storeroom	strawberry	swordfish	turtledove	warehouse

ACTIVITY 127 Form Compound Words

Name:_____

Date:_____

Combine each word with other words to form at least three compound words. The word listed can be the first or second half of the compound word. Use a dictionary if you need ideas.

Examples: **ball** baseball   ballgame   ballroom   football

1. where _____
2. car _____
3. day _____
4. every _____
5. house _____
6. rain _____
7. room _____
8. some _____

Make a copy of a page from a newspaper or magazine. Find and circle all the compound words on the page. List the compound words you found on another sheet of paper.

ACTIVITY 128 Write Alliterative Sentences Using Compound Words

Name:_____

Date:_____

Alliteration is the use of several words together that begin with the same sound.
Example: Redheaded Rosemary raised ripe raspberries.

For each compound word, write a short alliterative sentence. Use at least three words that begin with the same letter as the compound word. Use a dictionary if you aren't sure of the meaning of a word.

1. hedgehog _____
_____

2. daydream _____
_____

3. mailman _____
_____

4. pinpoint _____
_____

5. firefly _____
_____

ACTIVITY 129   Capitalize Proper Nouns

Name:_____

Date:_____

Capitalize proper nouns according
to the following rules:

Write another example.
Use a reference source if you need help.

Capitalize the first, middle, and last names of people.

Frank Lloyd Wright   _____

Capitalize the names of characters in books and movies.

the Mad Hatter   _____

Capitalize the specific names of animals.

Wilbur the pig; Wendell the Wonder Dog   _____

Capitalize titles if they come before a name and are part of the name.

My doctor is Doctor Bowen.

Professor Jenkins is a doctor.   _____

Capitalize words naming relatives if they come directly before a name.

Uncle Bill sent me an e-mail.

Bill is my favorite uncle.   _____

Capitalize the first word and all important words of specific places and things.

the Isle of Man; the Sea of Cortez   _____

ACTIVITY 130   Capitalization

Name:_____

Date:_____

1. Write the first, last, and middle names of anyone: _____

2. Write the name of a museum: _____

3. Write the name of your school: _____

4. Write the name of a relative: _____

Rewrite each item correctly.

5. my aunt, grace _____

6. george, the professor _____

7. uncle jacob _____

8. south carolina _____

9. wanda, the fish _____

10. museum of modern art _____

11. the declaration of independence _____

ACTIVITY 131 | Capitalize and Italicize

Name:_____

Date:_____

Capitalize the first word and all important words in the names of...

books: *Alice's Adventures in Wonderland*
movies: *Indiana Jones and the Temple of Doom*
magazines and newspapers: *USA Today; Reader's Digest*
plays: *All's Well that Ends Well*
ships, trains, airplanes, and space shuttles: USS *Constitution, Challenger*

Do not capitalize short words like *a, an, the, in, out, or, and,* or *of* unless they are the first or last word in a title. When you type, use italics for titles of books, newspapers, magazines, plays, and movies. Since you can't write in italics, underline instead.

1. Write the title of the last book you read. _____
2. Name a local newspaper. _____
3. What magazine do you enjoy reading? _____
4. Name a play. _____
5. Write the title of a picture book. _____
6. What is your all-time favorite movie? _____
7. Write the name of any ship, train, airplane, or space shuttle. _____

ACTIVITY 132 | Capitalize and Use Quotation Marks

Name:_____

Date:_____

Use **quotation marks** and **capitalize** important words in the titles of...

songs: "The Yellow Rose of Texas"   **poems:** "Jabberwocky"
stories: "The City Mouse and the Country Mouse"   **TV shows:** "Wheel of Fortune"
articles in newspapers, magazines, and encyclopedias: "Superbowl Contenders"
chapters of books: "Advice from a Caterpillar"

Write an example of each type. Use correct capitalization and punctuation.

1. song _____
2. magazine article _____
3. story _____
4. poem _____
5. TV show _____
6. chapter in a book _____
7. encyclopedia article _____
8. newspaper article _____

ACTIVITY 133 · Words to Capitalize

Name:_____

Date:_____

Capitalize the first word and all important words in the names of...

Write another example.
Use a reference source if you need help.

holidays:
Chinese New Year

_____

trade names and product names:
Hewlett Packard™

_____

names of streets:
Wisconsin Avenue

_____

days of the week:
Wednesday

_____

months of the year (but not seasons):
September

_____

names of historic eras:
the Reformation

_____

planets, stars, solar systems, and galaxies:
Jupiter; Andromeda Galaxy

_____

ACTIVITY 134 · Words to Capitalize

Name:_____

Date:_____

Capitalize the first word and all important words in the names of...

Write another example.
Use a reference source if you need help.

political parties:
Whig Party

_____

schools, colleges, and universities:
University of Arizona

_____

monuments:
the Liberty Bell

_____

wars:
War of 1812

_____

battles:
Battle of Manassas

_____

government departments:
Department of Health and
Human Services

_____

famous documents:
Treaty of Ghent

_____

parks:
Yellowstone National Park

_____

ACTIVITY 135 Words to Capitalize

Name:_____

Date:_____

Capitalize the first word and all important words in the names of...

Write another example.
Use a reference source if you need help.

religious groups:
　Greek Orthodox

_____

deities:
　Apollo

_____

groups or clubs:
　Campfire Girls

_____

famous buildings and bridges:
　Hancock Building; Brooklyn Bridge

_____

mountains:
　Ozark Mountains

_____

landmarks:
　Chimney Rock

_____

bodies of water, including rivers, oceans, lakes, and seas:
　the Amazon River; the Indian Ocean;
　Lake Champlain; the Sea of Galilee

_____

ACTIVITY 136 Use Capitalization and Punctuation in Letter Writing

Name:_____

Date:_____

Capitalize all important words in the greeting of a letter.
Use a comma after the greeting in a friendly letter.
Capitalize only the first word in the closing of a letter.
Use a comma after the closing of a letter.

Example:

Dear Herman,

Yours truly,

Write a short letter inviting a relative to a holiday celebration. Include the name of the holiday, the day and month of the celebration, a greeting, and a closing.

_____,

_____

_____

_____

_____

_____

_____,

_____

ACTIVITY 137   Write Proper Adjectives

Name:_____

Date:_____

Proper adjectives are words that come from proper nouns.
    A person from Columbia is a <u>Columbian</u> citizen.
    An actor in a Shakespeare play is a <u>Shakespearian</u> actor.
    A person from Spain speaks the <u>Spanish</u> language.
Always capitalize proper adjectives.

Write the proper adjectives described below. Use a dictionary if you need help.

1. People in France speak the _____ language.
2. A person from Africa is _____.
3. A person from Japan is _____.
4. People in Switzerland make _____ chocolate.
5. A person from Finland is _____.
6. A person from Iraq is _____.
7. People in England speak the _____ language.
8. A person from Canada is _____.
9. A person from Slovakia is _____.
10. People who live in Hawaii are _____.

ACTIVITY 138   Identify Capitalization Errors

Name:_____

Date:_____

To **proofread** means to read carefully to find and correct all errors.

Proofread the sentences. Circle all the capitalization errors, and write in the correct capital letter above each error.

1. For breakfast, Tina ordered a denver omelet with swiss cheese and canadian bacon.
2. She drank a cup of english breakfast tea and a glass of florida orange juice.
3. Brad ate new england clam chowder and a lettuce salad with russian dressing, bermuda onions, and roma tomatoes for lunch.
4. Emily couldn't decide between the italian spaghetti with meat sauce and the broiled maine lobster.
5. Which type of sandwich do you like best: swedish meatballs on italian bread, polish sausage on german rye, philly cheese steak, or greek gyros?
6. I like boston cream pie, french vanilla ice cream, and georgia peach pie, but I like german chocolate cake best of all.

ACTIVITY 139   Review Capitalization/ Word Search

Name:_____

Date:_____

All important words in the items listed should be capitalized.

Circle the words listed below in the word search puzzle. Words may be printed vertically, backward, forward, and diagonally in the puzzle.

Battles	Books	Cities
Colleges	Days	Documents
Lakes	Months	Monuments
Mountains	Movies	Names
Oceans	Parks	Planets
Poems	Rivers	Schools
Seas	Ships	Songs
States	Stories	Valleys
Wars		

```
S G N O S M S H I P S S
T E S P O E M S L L E S
A T G N O S S P A L T O
T S T E N P E Y S N T R
E H T A L I I A T E T I
S R E N T L V D N T A E
L C I I E A O A E S B E
O S C V L M M C M R P S
O D Y L E E U K U A A E
H H E E S R L C N W R A
C Y L A K E S B O O K S
S N I A T N U O M D S O
```

ACTIVITY 140   Use Correct Capitalization and Punctuation/Write an Editorial

Name:_____

Date:_____

When people feel strongly about issues, they can express their opinions by writing **editorials** to newspapers or magazines.

A well-written editorial...
- Begins with an interesting topic sentence to catch the reader's attention.
- Clearly explains the issue.
- States how the writer feels about the issue.
- Provides specific examples or facts to support that opinion.
- Ends with a sentence that summarizes the main points the writer made.

On another sheet of paper, write an editorial. Use correct capitalization and punctuation. When you finish, trade papers with a partner and proofread. Make corrections. Rewrite your editorial.

Optional: Send your editorial to your school newspaper or a local newspaper.

ACTIVITY 141 Review Capitalization   Name:_____

Correct all capitalization errors, and rewrite the sentences.   Date:_____

1. when i was young, my favorite book was *little women* by louisa may alcott.

_____

_____

2. former members of the house of representatives include john quincy adams, john rainy, and shirley chisholm.

_____

_____

Many foods we eat include words with city or country names, such as Belgian waffles, Swiss cheese, and Polish pickles. There are also many nonfood items with city or country names, such as Mexican pottery and Venetian lace.

3. Write the names of other foods that include place names.

_____

_____

4. Write the names of other nonfood items that include place names.

_____

_____

ACTIVITY 142 Review Capitalization   Name:_____

Date:_____

1. Name a book you would like to read.

_____

2. What is your favorite holiday? _____

3. What is the name of a character in your favorite book? _____

4. Where would you like to go on vacation? _____

5. Name your favorite TV show. _____

6. What day is it today? _____

7. What month is your birthday? _____

8. Write your complete address. _____

_____

9. Write the name of a relative. _____

10. Write the name of your doctor or dentist. _____

11. Write the name of a landmark or body of water. _____

12. Write the brand name of a product you use. _____

ACTIVITY 143   Use Commas Correctly

Name:_____

Date:_____

- Use a comma to separate three or more words in a list.
- Use a comma between the name of a city and state.
- Use a comma between the name of a city and country.
- Use a comma to separate the day from the date.
- Use a comma to separate the date from the year.
- No comma is used if only the month and year are written.

hop, skip, and jump
Madison, Wisconsin
Toronto, Canada
Tuesday, December 16
Friday, December 25, 1891
October 1492

1. Write the day, date, month, and year you were born. _____

2. Write today's day, date, month, and year. _____

3. Complete the sentence by listing six things you like to eat. Use commas as needed.

   I like _____ _____ _____

   _____ _____ and _____.

4. In what city and state do you live? _____

5. List the name of any state and its capital. _____

6. What city and country would you like to visit? _____

ACTIVITY 144   Use Capitalization and Commas in Context/Write a Letter

Name:_____

Date:_____

Write a short letter to the author of a book you like. Remember to use correct capitalization and punctuation in your letter.

_____
(Today's date)

Dear _____

_____

_____

_____

_____

_____

_____
(Closing)

_____
(Your name)

ACTIVITY 145 Use Commas Correctly

Name:_____

Date:_____

- Use a comma after an introductory phrase in a sentence.
- Use a comma to set off nouns in direct address.

- Use a comma to set off appositives.

- Use a comma to set off words that interrupt the flow of the sentence.

Yes, I can do that.
Could you lend me
your book, Amy?
My sister, who is 12,
was born on May 6.
The band, which was too loud,
hurt my ears.

Add commas where needed.

1. So what do you think Brad?

2. Chad are your aunts uncles and cousins coming to the reunion?

3. The baby giraffes who were over six feet tall looked awkward.

4. No Carmen I can't attend the concert on Friday July 7.

5. Unfortunately we will be in Taos New Mexico on vacation then.

6. My grandparents Esther and Lee moved to Naples Florida.

ACTIVITY 146 Review Comma Usage

Name:_____

Rewrite the dates using commas and correct capitalization.

Date:_____

1. wednesday december 15 1948   _____

2. january 1873   _____

3. friday october 12 1492   _____

4. february 14 2114   _____

Match how commas are used with the examples.

5. _____ to separate day, date, and year

6. _____ after the greeting in a letter

7. _____ after the closing in a letter

8. _____ to separate words in a list

9. _____ between a city and state

10. _____ between a city and country

11. _____ to separate words in direct address

12. _____ to separate appositives

13. _____ after an introductory phrase

a. Alice, the girl in the story, followed the rabbit.

b. Santa Claus, Georgia

c. Dear Mock Turtle,

d. Yes, we enjoyed reading about her adventures.

e. tea, crumpets, and watercress sandwiches

f. Your friend, the Cheshire Cat

g. Alice, watch out for that rabbit hole!

h. Cadbury, England

i. Friday, July 13, 1313

ACTIVITY 147   Use Semicolons Correctly

Name: _____

Date: _____

A **semicolon** signals a pause longer than for a comma but not as long as for a period. Semicolons are used between closely related independent clauses not joined by *and, or, nor, for, yet,* or *but.* An **independent clause** contains a complete idea and can stand alone.

Example: Brian was outgoing; his sister was shy.

Add semicolons to punctuate these sentences correctly. Some sentences require more than one semicolon.

1. Jean wanted soda Sal asked for lemonade.
2. I got up early my brother slept until noon.
3. "I came I saw I conquered," is a famous quote by Julius Caesar.
4. Jessie reads adventure novels she also likes science fiction.
5. The ship traveled over the rough sea Sean was sick.
6. I tried I failed I tried again.
7. The boys went to the ballgame the girls decided to see a movie instead.
8. Rachel wore red Wendy wore white Beth wore blue.

ACTIVITY 148   Use Semicolons in Context/Write Independent Clauses

Name: _____

Date: _____

Add a semicolon and an independent clause to complete the sentences. Remember, do not use a conjunction with a semicolon. An independent clause can stand alone as a complete sentence.

1. I lost my wallet _____.
2. _____ Mia jumped over the net.
3. Jogging is good exercise _____.
4. The sirens blared _____.
5. My bike tire looked flat _____.
6. _____

   Shelly preferred Limburger cheese.
7. _____

   the band played on and on.
8. The storm broke _____.

74

ACTIVITY 149 Use Colons Correctly

Name:_____

Date:_____

Use a **colon**...

- after the greeting in a business letter.   Dear Professor:

- between the hour and the minute when showing time.   11:37 A.M.

- between the volume and page number of a periodical.   Time 14:11

- between chapters and verses of the Bible.   Genesis 2:9

- before a list of three or more items.
    Please buy these fruits: limes, lemons, apples, bananas, and pineapples.

- to introduce a long statement or quotation.
    John F. Kennedy said: "My fellow Americans, ask not what your country can do for you —ask what can you do for your country. My fellow citizens of the world, ask not what America will do for you, but what together we can do for the freedom of man."

Add colons where needed in the sentences below. Some sentences could require more than one colon.

1. Dear Doctor Preston

2. We are currently sold out of these items waders, creels, and silly hats.

3. Our store is open daily until 9 15 P.M.

4. The following quotation is from Proverbs 1 1 "A good name is more desirable than great riches,…"

ACTIVITY 150 Review Usage of Semicolons and Colons

Name:_____

Date:_____

If the colon and/or semicolon is used correctly in the sentence, write "C."
If not, write "X" and correct it.

1. _____ Benjamin Franklin had many talents: author, printer, inventor, scientist, and diplomat.

2. _____ Which of these items were not invented by Benjamin Franklin; the lightning rod, bifocals, the odometer, or electricity?

3. _____ Franklin published the *Pennsylvania Gazette* he wrote *Poor Richard: An Almanack.*

4. _____ Dear Mr. Franklin;

5. _____ Could you meet me at the courthouse at 10:15 tomorrow morning?

6. _____ Franklin was a diplomat he helped sign a treaty with France.

7. _____ Did Franklin sign; the Declaration of Independence or the Constitution?

8. _____ Check out the quotations in *Poor Richard: An Almanack 3:31.*

ACTIVITY 151 Use Quotation Marks and Commas in Dialogue

Name: _____

Date: _____

Quotation marks enclose the words someone says in a sentence. The parts of a sentence with quotation marks are separated by a comma or other punctuation. If the words of the speaker are a question, include the question mark inside the quotation marks.

Examples: Zelda asked, "Would you like to come over after school tomorrow?"
                "Sounds good to me," Jan replied.

Underline the words that tell who is speaking. Put quotation marks around the words spoken.

1. Where are you going? Jim asked.
2. Joel replied, I'm headed over to school for football practice.
3. Have you met the new coach yet? asked Jim.
4. Not yet. We'll meet him today, replied Joel.
5. I heard he was pretty tough, Jim stated.
6. I heard that too, Joel said.
7. We need someone to get our team in shape, explained Joel.
8. Last year we were 1 and 11, Joel continued.
9. That's pitiful! exclaimed Jim.

ACTIVITY 152 Use Contractions in Context/Write Dialogue

Name: _____

Date: _____

Write dialogue using correct punctuation. Include at least one contraction in each sentence.

1. _____ asked Toby.

2. _____ Tyler replied.

3. _____ said Toby.

4. Tyler answered _____

5. Toby said _____

6. _____ shouted Tyler.

7. _____ Toby asked.

8. Tyler whispered _____

9. _____ Toby agreed.

ACTIVITY 153 Use Quotation Marks and Commas in Dialogue

Name: _____

Date: _____

More than one set of quotation marks can be used in a sentence.
Example: "Oh," said Sara, "I didn't know that."

Add punctuation. Put quotation marks around the words spoken.

1. Did you hear about the twins, Jack and Jill asked Peter
2. No replied Willie. What happened
3. They had a bad fall he said, down the big hill north of town
4. What were they doing on the hill asked Willie. It's pretty steep
5. I heard they went up there to fetch some water Peter said, but I don't believe that. Who would climb all the way up a hill just for a pail of water
6. It could be true Willie said. You know how Jill is about using only well water for her garden
7. She says that's how she gets those exotic flowers to grow so well Willie told Peter
8. I don't care much for those silver bells and cockle shells she grows he said, but I must admit that she grows the best pumpkins and peppers in town

ACTIVITY 154 Use Quotation Marks and Commas in Context/Write Dialogue

Name: _____

Date: _____

Write a conversation between characters in any nursery rhyme such as "Peter, Peter, Pumpkin Eater," "Hey, Diddle Diddle," "Little Bo Peep," "Humpty Dumpty," "Little Miss Muffet," or "Hickory, Dickory, Dock."

Remember to use quotation marks, commas, and other punctuation.

_____

_____

_____

_____

_____

_____

_____

Continue on another sheet of paper if you need more space to write.

ACTIVITY 155 Punctuate Abbreviations

Name:_____

Date:_____

Abbreviations are shortened forms of words. Use a period after most abbreviations. If the word should be capitalized, capitalize the abbreviation.
Examples: General: Gen.   October: Oct.   fluid ounces: fl. oz.

Match the words with their abbreviations. Use a dictionary if you are not sure.

1. _____ Lieutenant	11. _____ Avenue	a. Hwy.	k. lb.
2. _____ Doctor	12. _____ Highway	b. Col.	l. Lt.
3. _____ foot or feet	13. _____ inch or inches	c. in.	m. Sgt.
4. _____ February	14. _____ Sergeant	d. Ave.	n. Jr.
5. _____ Mister	15. _____ pound	e. St.	o. Dr.
6. _____ Mount/Mountain	16. _____ Colonel	f. Mr.	p. Rev.
7. _____ Junior	17. _____ Friday	g. oz.	q. tsp.
8. _____ Street or Saint	18. _____ Boulevard	h. ft.	r. Feb.
9. _____ Reverend	19. _____ teaspoon	i. Mt.	s. Blvd.
10. _____ ounce	20. _____ cup or cups	j. Fri.	t. c.

ACTIVITY 156 Punctuate Initials and Abbreviations

Name:_____

Date:_____

An **initial** is the first letter of someone's name. Use a period after a person's initials.
Examples: P. T. Barnum   J. K. Rowling
If an abbreviation is the last word in a sentence that ends in a period, use only one period. If an abbreviation is the last word in a sentence that ends with a question mark or exclamation mark, use the period for the abbreviation plus the end sentence punctuation.
Examples: She arrives on Fri.   Will you meet her on Fri.?

Add punctuation to correct the sentences.

1. E B White wrote *Charlotte's Web*

2. A A Milne wrote stories about Winnie-the-Pooh and his friends

3. An accident on Mon closed Hwy 41 for six hrs

4. Can you tell me how to get to Sesame St

5. I can meet you on Tues at the corner of Diamond Dr and Acorn Ave

6. Mr Rogers came in last in the 100-yd dash

7. Would you like to go to St Louis on Sun

8. J J Johnson, Jr, was 19 in long and weighed 7 lbs and 14 oz

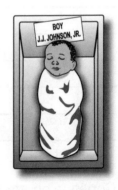

ACTIVITY 157 Abbreviations Without Periods

Name:_____

Date:_____

Do not use a period at the end of abbreviations for single words if all words in the abbreviation are capitalized.

Examples: TV (television)   GB (gigabytes)   C (centigrade)   F (Fahrenheit)

The official abbreviation for every U.S. state contains only two letters. Both letters are capitalized. No periods are used after the abbreviations, even if the name of the state contains two words, such as New Jersey and West Virginia.

Use a map, the U.S. Postal Service website, or another reference source to find the state abbreviations. http://www.usps.com/ncsc/lookups/abbreviations.html

Write the abbreviations for these states.   Write the name of the state for each abbreviation.

1. The state where you live _____   5. AZ _____

2. Michigan   _____   6. LA _____

3. Maryland   _____   7. NE _____

4. Delaware   _____   8. NJ _____

Cut an article from an old newspaper or magazine. Circle the proper nouns in the article. Underline all the abbreviations. Make lists of the proper nouns and the abbreviations on another sheet of paper.

ACTIVITY 158 Use Correct Capitalization and Punctuation/Sentence Writing

Name:_____

Date:_____

1. Write a sentence that includes a semicolon. _____

_____

2. Write a sentence that includes two or more abbreviations. _____

_____

3. Write a sentence that includes a colon and two or more commas. _____

_____

4. Write a sentence that uses a question mark and more than two abbreviations.

_____

5. Write a sentence that uses two or more abbreviations that do not end in a period.

_____

6. Write a sentence that uses two sets of quotation marks. _____

_____

_____

ACTIVITY 159 Review Capitalization and Punctuation/Test-Taking

Name:_____

Date:_____

Write "T" for true or "F" for false.

1. _____ Capitalize adjectives that come from proper nouns.
2. _____ If an abbreviation is the last word in a sentence that ends with a question mark or exclamation point, use the period for an abbreviation plus the end of sentence punctuation.
3. _____ Use italics or underline names of books, newspapers, magazines, plays, and movies.
4. _____ Capitalize important words in names of newspapers and magazines.
5. _____ If an abbreviation is the last word in a sentence that ends in a period, use two periods.
6. _____ Use a comma between chapters and verses of the Bible.
7. _____ The official abbreviation for every U.S. state contains two letters followed by a period.
8. _____ Capitalize short words like *a, an, the, in, or, and,* or *of* when they are part of a title.
9. _____ Use quotation marks and capitalize all words said by someone.
10. _____ Never use more than one set of quotation marks in a single sentence.

ACTIVITY 160 Review Capitalization and Punctuation/Test-Taking

Name:_____

Date:_____

Write "T" for true or "F" for false.

1. _____ Capitalize all important words in the greeting of a letter.
2. _____ Use an apostrophe in contractions to show where letters have been omitted.
3. _____ Use a semicolon after the greeting in a friendly letter.
4. _____ Use a colon after the greeting in a business letter.
5. _____ Use a comma after the closing in a letter.
6. _____ An independent clause contains a complete idea and can stand alone.
7. _____ Use commas to set off words in direct address.
8. _____ Use a period after most abbreviations.
9. _____ Use a semicolon between the hour and the minute when showing time.
10. _____ Use a colon between the volume and page number of a periodical.
11. _____ Use a period before a list of three or more items.
12. _____ Use a colon to introduce a long statement or quotation.
13. _____ A semicolon signals a pause longer than for a comma, but not as long as a period.
14. _____ Use a semicolon between closely related independent clauses not joined by conjunctions.

ACTIVITY 161 Write Acronyms

Name:_____

Date:_____

Acronyms are words made from the first letters of a group of words. Usually, the word is pronounced by saying the name of each letter. Capitalize all letters in acronyms. Do not use periods.
Example: NBA stands for the National Basketball Association.

Use a dictionary or other reference source to write the acronyms.

Acronym	Meaning
1. _____	absent without leave
2. _____	Internal Revenue Service
3. _____	also known as
4. _____	American Broadcasting Company
5. _____	Greenwich Mean Time
6. _____	registered nurse
7. _____	recreational vehicle
8. _____	amplitude modulation
9. _____	United States Marine Corps
10. _____	sport utility vehicle

ACTIVITY 162 Write Meanings of Acronyms

Name:_____

Date:_____

Acronyms are words made from the first letters of a group of words. We use acronyms in our everyday communications, both written and oral. If you turn on CNN or ESPN, you might hear the announcer mention the CIA or NHL. Understanding common acronyms helps us become better communicators.

Use a dictionary or other reference source to find the meaning of each of these acronyms.

1. FM _____
2. MP _____
3. VFW _____
4. MTV _____
5. CNN _____
6. NFL _____
7. DVD _____
8. PTA _____
9. WHO _____
10. USAF _____
11. OPEC _____
12. NATO _____
13. YMCA _____
14. UNICEF _____

Answer Keys

Activity 1 (p. 1)
Answers will vary.

Activity 2 (p. 1)
1. Joey = P; grandparents = C;
   Sidney, Australia = P
2. grandparents = C; March = P
3. Australia = P; continent = C;
   equator = C
4. octopus = C; reefs = C; coast = C
5. Joey = P; kangaroos, wombats,
   bandicoots, dingoes, platypus,
   devil, visit = C

Activity 3 (p. 2)
Answers will vary. Check for correctness
and capitalization.

Activity 4 (p. 2)
Sentences will vary.

Activity 5 (p. 3)
1. A   2. C   3. A
4. A   5. C   6. C
7. C   8. A   9. C
10. C   11. A   12. A
Sentences will vary.

Activity 6 (p. 3)
Common: property; weather; ceiling;
terror; chills; people; wizard; pins;
turtles; world; wand; wisdom; poverty;
worries
Proper: Cecelia; William; Terry; Tuesday
Concrete: Cecelia; property; ceiling;
William; Terry; chills; people; wizard;
pins; turtles; world; wand
Abstract: weather; terror; wisdom;
Tuesday; poverty; worries

Activity 7 (p. 4)
1. cousin (found)
2. snake (shed)
3. snakes (hatch)
4. Kay (wrote; directed)
5. audience (stood; clapped)
6. Everyone (enjoyed)
7. Wendy (watched); walrus (waddle)
8. Joe (Did hit)
9. ostriches (can fly)

Activity 8 (p. 4)
Answers will vary.

Activity 9 (p. 5)
1. I will (or shall) go to New York.
2. They will (or shall) sing in the
   chorus.

3. I will (or shall) take my hamster for
   a walk.
4. The engineers will (or shall) fix the
   problem.
5. Flowers will (or shall) grow in my
   garden.

Activity 10 (p. 5)
Answers will vary.

Activity 11 (p. 6)
Answers will vary. Check that verbs used
are inactive and fit in the sentences.

Activity 12 (p. 6)
Answers will vary. Check that students
used linking verbs.

Activity 13 (p. 7)
1. look   2. seemed
3. appeared   4. sounded
5. taste   6. felt
7. smelled   8. looked

Activity 14 (p. 7)
Answers will vary. Answers should be
adjectives.

Activity 15 (p. 8)
1. felt, A   2. felt, I   3. sounded, A
4. sounded, I 5. ran, A 6. grow, A
7. grew, I   8. sounded, I
9. appeared, A   10. seemed, I
11. smelled, A   12. smelled, I

Activity 16 (p. 8)
1. yes   2. yes   3. no
4. no   5. yes   6. no
7. no   8. no   9. yes
10. no   11. no   12. no
13. yes   14. no

Activity 17 (p. 9)
Sentences will vary.

Activity 18 (p. 9)
Some variation may occur.
Use an exclamation point after 1, 3, 5,
6, and 8.
Use a period after 2, 4, 7, 9, and 10.

Activity 19 (p. 10)
Sentences will vary.

Activity 20 (p. 10)
1. ? 2. . 3. ? 4. . 5. ! 6. .
7. T 8. F 9. T 10. F 11. F 12. T
Sentences will vary.

Activity 21 (p. 11)
1. Carla (painted the bedroom, kitchen,
   and bathroom.)
2. After he slept for nine hours, Jason
   (felt much better.)
3. After lunch, Tori and Emily (went
   swimming.)
4. My grandmother (wore a large straw
   hat in the garden.)
5. Silver bells and cockle shells (grow
   in Mary's garden.)
6. (Can) a hamster (learn to do
   tricks?)

Activity 22 (p. 11)
Answers will vary.

Activity 23 (p. 12)
1. stars   2. steps
3. seagulls   4. sparrows
5. suns   6. sons
7. sounds   8. shirts
9. wishes   10. fusses
11. dishes   12. brushes
13. arches   14. benches
15. taxes   16. grasses

Activity 24 (p. 12)
1. canaries   2. buddies
3. flies   4. stories
5. delays   6. arrays
7. Tuesdays   8. guppies
9. ways   10. ponies
11. ladies   12. toys
13. cries   14. dandies
15. fries   16. dyes

Activity 25 (p. 13)
1. lives   2. heroes   3. mice
4. scarves 5. cattle   6. scissors
7. people   8. potatoes 9. teeth
10. jeans   11. elves   12. deer
13. oxen   14. leaves   15. knives
16. loaves

Activity 26 (p. 13)
Answers will vary. Check spelling.

Activity 27 (p. 14)
1. sigh   2. wishes   3. runs
4. roar   5. grow   6. falls
7. answer

Activity 28 (p. 14)
1. S – band   2. S – audience
3. P – children   4. S – journey
5. S – roof 6. P – brothers and I
7. S – door   8. P – ducks
9. S – it   10. S – brother
Verbs will vary.

Activity 29 (p. 15)
1. tries   2. wishes   3. chases
4. buzzes   5. waxes   6. fishes
7. passes   8. says   9. boxes
10. hatches

Activity 30 (p. 15)
Both answers are no. Explanations will vary.

Activity 31 (p. 16)

Present Tense	Past Tense
1. bend	bent
2. bind	bound
3. buy	bought
4. catch	caught
5. bite	bit
6. blow	blew
7. break	broke
8. build	built
9. dig	dug
10. deal	dealt
11. say	said
12. send	sent
13. shake	shook
14. eat	ate
15. tear	tore
16. tell	told
17. feed	fed
18. fight	fought
19. find	found
20. wear	wore

Activity 32 (p. 16)

Present Tense	Past Tense
1. fling	flung
2. forget	forgot
3. forgive	forgave
4. fall	fell
5. go	went
6. grow	grew
7. have or has	had
8. keep	kept
9. lead	led
10. leave	left
11. sweep	swept
12. swing	swung
13. mean	meant
14. sit	sat
15. ring	rang
16. spend	spent
17. arise	arose
18. awake	awoke
19. become	became
20. speak	spoke

Activity 33 (p. 17)
Sentences will vary. Past tense is listed.
1. bet   2. blew   3. burned or burnt
4. cast   5. caught   6. cost   7. cut
8. let   9. put

Activity 34 (p. 17)
1. drank   drunk
2. thought   thought
3. knew   known
4. wore   worn
5. cut   cut
6. brought   brought
7. swam   swum

Activity 35 (p. 18)
1. spends   2. will rise
3. have or had caught 4. will set
5. keep   6. means
7. have or had put   8. built
9. will rid   10. cut
11. feeds
12. have or had mown or mowed
13. will swing   14. buy
15. will sink
16. have or had grown

Activity 36 (p. 18)
1. will go: future
2. enjoys: present
3. had moved; past participle
4. Do like: present
5. prefer: present
6. had visited: past participle
7. go: present
8. works: present
9. will giggle
10. chucked
11. have or had swollen

Activity 37 (p. 19)
Answers will vary.

Activity 38 (p. 19)
1. proper; concrete
2. common; concrete
3. common; abstract
4. common; concrete
5. common; concrete; collective
6. common; abstract
7. common; abstract
8. proper; concrete
9. common; concrete; collective
10. common; concrete
11. proper; concrete
12. proper; concrete
13. proper; concrete

Activity 39 (p. 20)
1. h   2. i   3. m   4. j
5. k   6. n   7. f   8. d
9. e   10. l   11. a   12. g
13. c   14. b

Activity 40 (p. 20)
1. T   2. F   3. T   4. T
5. T   6. F   7. F   8. F
9. F   10. T   11. T   12. T

Activity 41 (p. 21)
1. I: Ishmael
2. We: the crew and Ishmael
3. He: Captain Ahab
4. He: Captain Ahab
5. it: storm
6. I: Ishmael
7. We: crew and Ishmael
8. you: the reader

Activity 42 (p. 21)
The pronoun *you* can be singular or plural. Always use a plural verb with *you*. Pronouns are listed. Nouns will vary.
1. He; I   2. We   3. We
4. They   5. It   6. It
7. He   8. You

Activity 43 (p. 22)
1. purple → finch; three and small → eggs; her → nest; tall and maple → tree
2. wrapping → paper; yellow, blue, and green → swirls; big and red → dots
3. new → coach; green → carpeting; gold, white, and team → logos
4. huge and oak → desk and bookcase; small → office
5. cheese, pepperoni, onion, and mushroom → pizza; garlic → breadsticks

Activity 44 (p. 22)
1. All → insects; hard → exoskeleton; three-part → body; three → pairs; jointed → legs; compound → eyes; two → antennae.
2. million and different → types
3. largest → insect; ancient → dragonfly
4. This, predatory, and flying → insect; prehistoric → times; two-foot → wingspan.
5. Male → crickets; loud and chirping → sound; their → forewings
6. praying → mantis; strong, barbed, and front → legs
7. interesting → insect

Activity 45 (p. 23)
Answers will vary.

Activity 46 (p. 23)
1. blue, brick, broad, blue, brick
2. Shy, seven, silly, sunny
3. Cheerful, cherry
4. caffeine, copper, coffee
5. Big, Boston, best, better, Big
6. chewy, cheddar, cheese

Tongue twisters and adjectives will vary.

Activity 47 (p. 24)
Sentences will vary.

Activity 48 (p. 24)
1. A   2. A   3. N   4. A
5. N   6. N   7. N   8. A

Sentences will vary.

Activity 49 (p. 25)
1. Over; in; of
2. with; down; across; through; to
3. with   4. for
5. by   6. to; in

Sentences will vary.

Activity 50 (p. 25)
1. in the (house); under the (rug); by the red (chair)
2. From the hot air (balloon); at the (buildings); across the (city); to the (river)
3. from the (town); across the (river); up the (mountain); into an (opening); in a (cave)
4. on (vacation); with our (camera); of the (mountains); across the (valley)
5. Without a (doubt); of the (rainbow); on (exhibit)
6. from (me); to (you); for your (birthday)
7. through the (jungle); across the (stream); over the rocky (plain); to its home (territory)

Activity 51 (p. 26)
Sentences 1, 4, 5, 6, 8, 9, and 10 do not contain prepositional phrases.
2. behind Amos   3. in line
7. to him

Activity 52 (p. 26)
Answers will vary.

Activity 53 (p. 27)
1. her   2. them   3. me
4. you   5. us   6. you   7. me

Activity 54 (p. 27)
Answers may vary. Be certain students use objective pronouns only.

Activity 55 (p. 28)
1. In for a penny; in for a pound
2. of one; of the other
3. to them   4. in time

Explanations will vary

Activity 56 (p. 28)
1. T   2. T   3. T   4. T
5. T   6. F   7. T   8. T
9. T   10. T   11. F   12. F
13. F 14. F   15. T

Activity 57 (p. 29)
1. her; me   2. glasses   3. them
4. book   5. paper   6. car; one
7. it   8. items   9. it
10. you   11. siren   12. nap

Activity 58 (p. 29)
Answers in blanks may vary. Be certain students write objective pronouns only.
1. O   2. D   3. D   4. D
5. D   6. D   7. O   8. D
9. O   10. D

Activity 59 (p. 30)
1. her; (A+)   2. me; (meal)
3. me; (secret)   4. him; (gift)
5. teacher; (project)
6. workers; (salary)
7. nephew; (ticket)
8. friend; (story)
9. students; (look)

Activity 60 (p. 30)
Entries will vary. Check that nouns and pronouns are used and labeled correctly.

Activity 61 (p. 31)
1. often   2. rarely; too
3. Sometimes; along   4. usually
5. early; seldom
6. Tomorrow; quickly; again
7. carefully   8. along

Activity 62 (p. 31)
1. flew quickly, silently
2. usually sleep
3. sleep deeply
4. can avoid easily
5. often sleep; usually feed
6. are actually
7. can't walk well
8. often welcome

Activity 63 (p. 32)
1. A   2. A   3. A   4. P
5. P   6. P   7. P   8. A
9. P   10. A

Activity 64 (p. 32)
Sentences will vary. Correct words are listed.
1. gratefully   2. fiercely
3. nervously   4. politely

Activity 65 (p. 33)
Answers will vary. Words used must be comparative forms of adjectives.

Activity 66 (p. 33)
Answers will vary. Words used must be superlative forms of adjectives.

Activity 67 (p. 34)
1. jollier; jolliest
2. fresher; freshest
3. more gorgeous; most gorgeous
4. more childish; most childish
5. wiser; wisest
6. None
7. drier; driest

Activity 68 (p. 34)
Sentences will vary. Correct forms of the words are listed.
1. farther   2. worst   3. most
4. more   5. best   6. less
7. better; best

Activity 69 (p. 35)
Answers may vary. Accept any of the adjectives listed as long as the correct form is used.

Activity 70 (p. 35)
1. fuzzy = P; pink = P;
   more shabby = C; (more) worn = C
2. brilliant = P; red = P;
   less spectacular = C;
   morning's = P; pink = P; purple = P
3. best = S; largest = S
4. mail = P; red = P; new = P
5. difficult = P; timely = P
6. Tin = P; best = S
7. Cowardly = P; more = C
8. most frightened = S; smartest = S
9. happy = P; new = P; happier = C
10. farther = C

Activity 71 (p. 36)
Use *more* and *most* with all adverbs except 3. very and 6. yesterday.

Activity 72 (p. 36)
Adverbs will vary. Verbs are listed.
1. ready   2. growls
3. will be   4. will arrive
5. cried   6. check
7. could eat   8. Can move
9. waited   10. looked
11. snores   12. Did sleep

Activity 73 (p. 37)
1. Good; to those
2. of the frying pan; into the fire
3. of a loaf; better
4. your; to them
5. All; no; dull
6. old; new
7. Inside every cloud; silver
8. in glass houses
9. of all evil
10. Great; from little acorns
Proverbs will vary.

Activity 74 (p. 37)
Answers will vary.

Activity 75 (p. 38)
Answers will vary.

Activity 76 (p. 38)
Answers will vary.

Activity 77 (p. 39)
1. because   2. so   3. but
4.–7. Answers will vary.

Activity 78 (p. 39)
Sentences will vary.

Activity 79 (p. 40)
Answers may vary. Check for reasonableness.

Activity 80 (p. 40)
Journals will vary.

Activity 81 (p. 41)
1. T   2. F   3. T   4. F
5. T   6. F   7. T   8. T
9. T   10. T   11. F   12. T

Activity 82 (p. 41)
1. adjectives   2. verbs
3. pronouns   4. verbs
5. common nouns
6. proper nouns   7. prepositions
8. conjunctions   9. adverbs
10. prepositions   11. adverbs
12. pronouns
13. common nouns

Activity 83 (p. 42)
1. Do you know where Todd went? I can't find him anywhere.
2. How can you eat that stinky cheese? I can't!
3. Look out! That water is very deep.
4. My hamster ran out the door. Did you see which way he went? Will he get lost?

5. The sky got darker, and the snow began to fall. The sidewalks were soon covered, and the roads became slippery.

Activity 84 (p. 42)
Answers will vary. Teacher check for proper use of parts of speech.

Activity 85 (p. 43)
1. What   2. Who   3. Which
4. Which   5. Which   6. What
7. What   8. which   9. who

Activity 86 (p. 43)
1. Who   2. who   3. whom
4. Whose   5. whom   6. What
7. whom   8. who   9. what
10. What

Activity 87 (p. 44)
Answers will vary. Check that sentence type and specified elements are present.

Activity 88 (p. 44)
1. – 7, and 10. – 12: Use 's
8. and 9: Use only the apostrophe

Activity 89 (p. 45)
1. wives'   2. men's   3. mice's
4. wolves'   5. people's   6. feet's
7. bunnies'   8. attorneys' 9. boxes'
10. geese's   11. volcanoes'
12. heroes'

Activity 90 (p. 45)
Answers will vary.

Activity 91 (p. 46)
1. her/hers   2. my/mine
3. his/his   4. our/ours
5. their/theirs

Activity 92 (p. 46)
Sentences will vary.

Activity 93 (p. 47)
Singular subjective pronouns: he; I; it; she; you
Plural subjective pronouns: they; we; you
Singular objective pronouns: her; him; it; me; you
Plural objective pronouns: them; us; you
Singular possessive pronouns: her; hers; his; its; my; mine; your; yours

Plural objective pronouns: our; ours; their; theirs; your; yours
Male pronouns: he; him; his
Female pronouns: her; hers; she

Activity 94 (p. 47)
1. Sara Simpson gave her sister singing lessons at her sister's house.
2. The two toads took their toadstools to their teacher.
3. Marvin married Mabel, and they moved to Miami where they lived in a motel for a month.
4. In September, Sam sold his stamps to his sister Sue.

Activity 95 (p. 48)
The usual answers are given. Answers may vary.
1. can't   2. Don't   3. doesn't
4. shouldn't 5. can't   6. Don't
Reasons will vary.

Activity 96 (p. 48)
Sentences will vary.

Activity 97 (p. 49)
Answers will vary.

Activity 98 (p. 49)
1. how's   2. how'll   3. that's
4. that's   5. there's   6. what'll
7. where's   8. where's   9. why'd
10. who's   11. who'd   12. how'd
13. let's   14. that'll   15. there're
16. what's   17. what's   18. where'd
19. when's   20. who's   21. who'll
22. why's
Sentences will vary.

Activity 99 (p. 50)
1. him   2. yew   3. wee
4. we   5. your   6. there's
7. they're   8. you're   9. there
10. its   11. hymn   12. you
13. ewe   14. theirs   15. aye
16. it's

Activity 100 (p. 50)
1. P   2. C, cat is   3. C, it is
4. C, check is   5. C, you are
6. C, you are   7. C, what is
8. C, nobody is   9. C, there is
10. C, two is; C, three is
11. C, there is; C, there is
12. C, bark is

Activity 101 (p. 51)
1. Alice, where are you going?
2. Well, dear, what do you have to say for yourself?
3. Listen up, class. Tomorrow, we will have a test.
4. Derek, would you like to meet me at the library?
5. I can help you, Raphael, but I'm afraid I can't help you too, Monica.
6. Alice and Fay, come to the principal's office at once.
7. Would you like to ride with Dad to the mall, Kay?
8. Did you, Paul, plant those purple petunias?
9. Alicia, you ate eight cookies. That's enough.
10. Attention, everyone. This is not a drill, class.

Activity 102 (p. 51)
1. What is the capital of Texas, <u>Austin or Houston</u>?
2. Tick Bite, <u>a town in North Carolina</u>, and Hot Coffee, <u>a town in Missis-sippi</u>, are two places with unusual names.
3. The green tree frog, <u>the official state amphibian of Georgia and Louisiana</u>, is a type of frog found in temperate and tropical areas throughout the world
4. Connecticut, <u>officially nicknamed the Constitution State</u>, is also known as the Nutmeg State.
5. No one seems to know why Indiana, <u>known as the Hoosier State</u>, has that nickname.
6. Milk, <u>the official state beverage of many states</u>, is better for you than soda.
7. Only one state, <u>Florida</u>, has orange juice as its official state beverage.
8. Cranberry juice, <u>the official state beverage of Massachusetts</u>, and tomato juice, <u>the state beverage of Ohio</u>, are unusual, but not as strange as the state soft drink of Nebraska.

Activity 103 (p. 52)
1. A – Potter, the boy who lived,
2. DA – fair, Charlotte
3. DA – tornado, Pecos Bill
4. A – Spiderman, originally a character in comic books,
5.–6. Sentences will vary.

Activity 104 (p. 52)
1. aren't	2. she'll	3. hasn't
4. I'll	5. they'll	6. wouldn't
7. he'd	8. you've	9. how's
10. who'll	11. was not	12. there is
13. do not	14. I would	
15. they have		16. that is
17. you would		18. are not
19. let us		20. will not

Activity 105 (p. 53)
1. adverbs		2. suffixes
3. suffixes		4. conjunctions
5. adjectives		6. adverbs
7. adverbs and adjectives		
8. proper nouns	9. appositives	
10. active verbs	11. contractions	
12. apostrophes	13. apostrophes	
14. prepositions		

Activity 106 (p. 53)
1. F	2. T	3. F	4. T
5. T	6. F	7. F	8. T
9. F	10. F	11. F	12. T
13. T	14. F		

Activity 107 (p. 54)
1. N	2. V	3. N	4. V
5. N	6. V	7. N	8. V
9. N	10. V	11. V	12. N

Activity 108 (p. 54)
Sentences will vary. Check that words are used as parts of speech indicated.

Activity 109 (p. 55)
Sentences will vary.

Activity 110 (p. 55)
Verbs: answer; arch; blend; blooms; brown; call; can; clean; clutch; coast; cook; dance; debate; design; digest; drop; duck; exhaust; experience; focus; frost; fuel; guard; hand; issue; latch; loom; offer; paint; pilot; plow; post; range; scoop; second; secure; sketch; sleep; sprout; stall; stock; stop; trip; type; water

Nouns: answer; arch; blend; blooms; brown; call; can; clutch; coast; commercial; complex; computer; cook; dance; debate; design; dice; digest; drop; duck; exhaust; experience; focus; frost; fuel; guard; hand; issue; latch; loom; offer; orange; paint; patient; pilot; plow; post; range; safe; scoop; second; sketch; sleep; sprout; stall; stock; stop; terminal; trial; trip; type; water

Adjectives: answer; arch; brown; call; clean; commercial; complex; computer; cook; dance; design; dice; duck; exhaust; frost; fuel; guard; hand; latch; orange; paint; patient; pilot; post; range; safe; scoop; second; secure; stock; stop; terminal; trial; water
Additional words will vary.

Activity 111 (p. 56)
Answers will vary.

Activity 112 (p. 56)
Answers will vary.

Activity 113 (p. 57)
Answers will vary.

Activity 114 (p. 57)
Answers will vary.

Activity 115 (p. 58)
Answers will vary.

Activity 116 (p. 58)
Answers will vary.

Activity 117 (p. 59)
1. unable, powerless, incapable
2. friendly, pleasant
3. careless, hasty
4. slow, leisurely, careful
5. certain, sure, definite
6. unkind, inconsiderate, mean
7. unaware, uninformed, ignorant
8. joyful, happy
9. squirm, wiggle
10. free, liberate
11. defiant, enemy
12. annoy, bother
13. interfere, pry, hinder
14. impose, require, inflict

Activity 118 (p. 59)
1. S	2. S	3. A	4. S
5. S	6. S	7. A	8. A
9. A	10. A	11. A	12. S
13. S	14. S	15. A	16. S
17. S	18. A	19. A	20. S
21. S	22. A	23. A	24. S

Activity 119 (p. 60)
1. buoy	2. boy	3. pries
4. principle	5. threw	6. bass
7. seize	8. through	9. bow
10. strait	11. base	12. principal
13. straight	14. prize	15. seas
16. beau		

Activity 120 (p. 60)
Answers will vary.
Homophones are listed.
1. ark   2. assent
3. bale   4. banned
5. bury   6. sell and cel
7. chilly   8. course
9. feet and fete   10. mite
11. roll   12. weight

Activity 121 (p. 61)
Answers will vary.

Activity 122 (p. 61)
Answers will vary.

Activity 123 (p. 62)
1. a   2. b   3. a   4. b
5. b   6. a   7. b   8. b
9. a   10. b   11. b   12. a
13. a   14. a

Activity 124 (p. 62)
1. b   2. a   3. a   4. b
5. b   6. c   7. b   8. c
9. b   10. a   11. c   12. a
13. b   14. b   15. a

Activity 125 (p. 63)
1. o   2. k   3. r   4. t
5. i   6. n   7. b   8. g
9. e   10. m   11. s   12. d
13. a   14. f   15. q   16. h
17. p   18. l   19. j   20. c

Activity 126 (p. 63)
Teacher check word division.
2. *Animals/Insects* (circled): bulldog, butterfly, firefly, hedgehog, inchworm, jellyfish, ladybug, polecat, rattlesnake, roadrunner, sapsucker, silkworm, swordfish, turtledove
3. *Food* (underlined): applesauce, cupcake, gooseberry, grapefruit, horseradish, meatloaf, oatmeal, pineapple, popcorn, potpie, shortcake, strawberry
4. *Places* (check marks): backyard, bedroom, courthouse, farmyard, greenhouse, Greenland, hallway, Hollywood, Iceland, lighthouse, Maryland, outhouse, Portland, storeroom, warehouse
5. elbow room

Activity 127 (p. 64)
Answers will vary. Some examples are given.
1. somewhere, elsewhere, nowhere, everywhere
2. carport, boxcar, railcar, handcar
3. everyday, Sunday, daylight, daybreak, someday
4. everyone, everyday, everywhere, everybody
5. houseboat, housefly, madhouse, house cat, housecoat
6. rainbow, raincoat, rainfall, rainwater
7. storeroom, bedroom, elbow room, roommate
8. someday, somewhere, someone, somebody, something

Activity 128 (p. 64)
Answers will vary.

Activity 129 (p. 65)
Answers will vary.

Activity 130 (p. 65)
1.–4. Answers will vary.
5. my aunt, Grace
6. George, the professor
7. Uncle Jacob
8. South Carolina
9. Wanda, the fish
10. Museum of Modern Art
11. the Declaration of Independence

Activity 131 (p. 66)
Answers will vary.

Activity 132 (p. 66)
Answers will vary.

Activity 133 (p. 67)
Answers will vary.

Activity 134 (p. 67)
Answers will vary.

Activity 135 (p. 68)
Answers will vary.

Activity 136 (p. 68)
Letters will vary.

Activity 137 (p. 69)
1. French   2. African
3. Japanese   4. Swiss
5. Finnish   6. Iraqi
7. English   8. Canadian
9. Slovakian   10. Hawaiian

Activity 138 (p. 69)
Words that should be capitalized are listed.
1. Denver; Swiss; Canadian
2. English; Florida
3. New England; Russian; Bermuda; Roma
4. Italian; Maine
5. Swedish; Italian; Polish; German; Philly; Greek
6. Boston; French; Georgia; German

Activity 139 (p. 70)

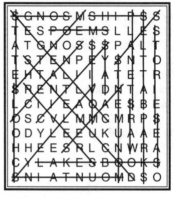

Seas may be found in two places.

Activity 140 (p. 70)
Editorials will vary.

Activity 141 (p. 71)
1. When I was young, my favorite book was *Little Women* by Louisa May Alcott.
2. Former members of the House of Representatives include John Quincy Adams, John Rainy, and Shirley Chisholm.
3.–4. Answers will vary.

Activity 142 (p. 71)
Answers will vary.

Activity 143 (p. 72)
Answers will vary.

Activity 144 (p. 72)
Letters will vary.

Activity 145 (p. 73)
1. So, what do you think, Brad?
2. Chad, are your aunts, uncles, and cousins coming to the reunion?
3. The baby giraffes, who were over six feel tall, looked awkward.
4. No, Carmen, I can't attend the concert on Friday, July 7.

5. Unfortunately, we will be in Taos, New Mexico, on vacation then.
6. My grandparents, Esther and Lee, moved to Naples, Florida.

Activity 146 (p. 73)
1. Wednesday, December 15, 1948
2. January 1873
3. Friday, October 12, 1492
4. February 14, 2114
5. i   6. c   7. f   8. e
9. b   10. h   11. g   12. a
13. d

Activity 147 (p. 74)
1. soda;   2. early;
3. I came; I saw; 4. novels;
5. sea;   6. I tried; I failed;
7. ballgame;
8. Rachel wore red; Wendy wore white;

Activity 148 (p. 74)
Answers will vary.

Activity 149 (p. 75)
1. Preston: 2. items:
3. 9:15
4. Add two colons— 1:1:

Activity 150 (p. 75)
1. C
2. Colon, not semicolon
3. Add semicolon after *Gazette*
4. Colon, not semicolon
5. C
6. Add semicolon after diplomat
7. Delete semicolon
8. C

Activity 151 (p. 76)
1. "Where are you going?" Jim asked.
2. Joel replied, "I'm headed over to school for football practice."
3. "Have you met the new coach yet?" asked Jim.
4. "Not yet. We'll meet him today," replied Joel.
5. "I heard he was pretty tough," Jim stated.
6. "I heard that too," Joel said.
7. "We need someone to get our team in shape," explained Joel.
8. "Last year we were 1 and 11," Joel continued.
9. "That's pitiful!" exclaimed Jim.

Activity 152 (p. 76)
Answers will vary.

Activity 153 (p. 77)
1. "Did you hear about the twins, Jack and Jill?" asked Peter.
2. "No," replied Willie. "What happened?"
3. "They had a bad fall," he said, "down the big hill north of town."
4. "What were they doing on the hill?" asked Willie. "It's pretty steep."
5. "I heard they went up there to fetch some water," Peter said, "but I don't believe that. Who would climb all the way up a hill just for a pail of water?"
6. "It could be true," Willie said. "You know how Jill is about using only well water for her garden."
7. "She says that's how she gets those exotic flowers to grow so well," Willie told Peter.
8. "I don't care much for those silver bells and cockle shells she grows," he said, "but I must admit that she grows the best pumpkins and peppers in town."

Activity 154 (p. 77)
Dialogues will vary.

Activity 155 (p. 78)
1. l   2. o   3. h   4. r
5. f   6. i   7. n   8. e
9. p   10. g   11. d   12. a
13. c   14. m   15. k   16. b
17. j   18. s   19. q   20. t

Activity 156 (p. 78)
1. E. B. White wrote *Charlotte's Web*.
2. A. A. Milne wrote stories about Winnie-the-Pooh and his friends.
3. An accident on Mon. closed Hwy. 41 for six hrs.
4. Can you tell me how to get to Sesame St.?
5. I can meet you on Tues. at the corner of Diamond Dr. and Acorn Ave.
6. Mr. Rogers came in last in the 100-yd. dash.
7. Would you like to go to St. Louis on Sun.?
8. J. J. Johnson, Jr., was 19 in. long and weighed 7 lbs. and 14 oz.

Activity 157 (p. 79)
1. Answer will vary.
2. MI   3. MD   4. DE
5. Arizona   6. Louisiana
7. Nebraska   8. New Jersey

Activity 158 (p. 79)
Sentences will vary.

Activity 159 (p. 80)
1. T   2. T   3. T   4. T
5. F   6. F   7. F   8. F
9. F   10. F

Activity 160 (p. 80)
1. T   2. T   3. F   4. T
5. T   6. T   7. T   8. T
9. F   10. T   11. F   12. T
13. T   14. T

Activity 161 (p. 81)
1. AWOL   2. IRS   3. AKA
4. ABC   5. GMT   6. RN
7. RV   8. AM   9. USMC
10. SUV

Activity 162 (p. 81)
1. frequency modulation
2. Military Police
3. Veterans of Foreign Wars
4. Music TV or Music Television
5. Cable News Network
6. National Football League
7. digital video disc
8. Parent-Teacher Association
9. World Health Organization
10. United States Air Force
11. Organization of Petroleum Exporting Countries
12. North Atlantic Treaty Organization
13. Young Men's Christian Association
14. United Nations International Children's Emergency Fund (now called the United Nations Children's Fund)